The Micro Cap Investor

The Micro Cap Investor

Strategies for Making Big Returns in Small Companies

RICHARD IMPERIALE

WILEY

John Wiley & Sons, Inc.

Published by John Wiley & Sons, Inc., Hoboken, New Jersey
Published simultaneously in Canada

For general information about our other products and services, please contact our Customer Care Department within the United States at 800-762-2974, outside the United States at 317-572-3993 or fax 317-572-4002.

Wiley also publishes its books in a variety of electronic formats. Some content that appears in print may not be available in electronic books. For more information about Wiley products, visit our web site at www.wiley.com.

Library of Congress Cataloging-in-Publication Data:

Imperiale, Richard, 1957–
  The micro cap investor : strategies for making big returns in small companies / Richard Imperiale.
      p. cm.
   Includes index.
   ISBN 0-471-47870-9 (cloth)
   1. Small capitalization stocks—United States.   2. Securities—United States.
  3. Portfolio management—United States.   I. Title.
   HG4971.I47 2005
   332.63'22—dc22

2004018701

Printed in the United States of America

10 9 8 7 6 5 4 3 2 1

Contents

Preface

This book is an explanation and analysis of micro cap stocks. These very small companies have endured a checkered history. In general terms, micro caps are large in absolute numbers but historically have been a small and misunderstood sector of the investment landscape. In this world of efficient markets and index funds, this perception has started to change. Many micro cap companies are well-managed, high-quality businesses that present an excellent investment opportunity. In addition, micro caps are a viable and competitive investment option for those who are looking to broaden and diversify their investment portfolios.

As a professional investor in micro cap stocks, I noticed that the average investor largely misunderstands these companies. Many professional investors and portfolio managers also have little knowledge or interest in micro caps. In addition, there are very few books or other resource materials on the subject of micro caps. Those books that are available are either very simple overviews of the subject or highly complex academic treatments of the topic. And most books do not address the fundamental research issues that underlie the basics of micro cap investing nor do they address the concept of how to integrate micro caps into an investment portfolio.

The Micro Cap Investor: Strategies for Making Big Returns in Small Companies is an attempt to address these very issues. The book begins by defining micro caps and reviewing why micro cap investors might be in a position to gain an information advantage. This is followed with a general discussion of micro caps as an asset class, an analysis of how micro caps behave as an investment class, and an explanation of how they are best integrated into an investor's portfolio.

The next three chapters of the book describe the fundamental economic issues that affect micro caps in general and attempt to analyze these issues in the context of the micro cap investment vehicle. The book continues with a series of case studies and a review of specific methods for analyzing and screening for micro cap investment opportunities. The final three chapters of the book use the theoretical constructs developed in the case studies to build a framework for investor action as well as reviewing the growth of PIPES, or private investments in public equities, a new capital financing opportunity for micro cap companies.

Micro caps are an emerging asset class. As in any new asset class, there is a limited amount of quality data available from which to draw conclusions. This book offers a practical and useful overview of the limited data that bridges theoretical constructs with practical investment knowledge. In addition, the book provides the reader with some practical statistical data relevant to the general analysis and valuation of the micro cap asset class. This appears in the numerous charts, tables, and graphs that summarize key micro cap data into a usable format.

My intention is for this book to fill a void in the available current literature about micro cap investing and to help supply a better understanding of an emerging asset class.

Richard Imperiale
Milwaukee, Wisconsin
September 27, 2004

Acknowledgments

Although the author ultimately gets credit for writing a book, there is an army of others who contribute to the process. I'd like to recognize them here.

This book is dedicated to my wife, Sue, and our two daughters, Emily and Mary, who put up with my absence at family and school functions and during many evenings and weekends. Their support and encouragement made the completion of this project possible. Every day they make me realize how fortunate I really am.

I'd like to thank my good friend and mentor, Dr. John Komives, from the Marquette University Business School. For the past 20 years we have worked together with a great sense of adventure on many business and academic projects. We have often discussed potential projects over a cold glass of beer on Friday evenings and this book is in part a result of those conversations.

Of course, it's not a book without a publisher. My friend and colleague Jerry Twedell, who is the author of several investment books, was kind enough to introduce me to his publisher, John Wiley & Sons. Through that introduction, I met David Pugh, who is now my editor at Wiley. In the middle of a less than favorable general investment climate, he was open-minded enough to listen to my ideas about micro caps, give me critical feedback, and go to bat for me on this project. David has been an excellent coach and critic, who helped me shape this book into a much better and more useful text. I now consider him a good friend and thank him for all his help.

I thought the writing was hard. But that was easy compared to the copyediting. For helping me get through that phase of the project I want to thank Ginny Carroll. When the writing was finally complete, the book was behind schedule. Ginny's talent and skill helped to get the project back on schedule. Through the editing process she also patiently taught me many useful lessons about editing and publishing that will make me a better writer in the future.

Much of the data in the book is compiled from academic papers, company reports, and industry trade associations. Much of that data was processed by my assistant, Rochell Tillman, and my research associate, Farid Sheikh. Their diligence and hard work have helped to provide consolidated data not found in any other single place.

I'd also like to thank Lyn Woloszyk, who transcribed many of the chapters and case studies for the book. She often did the transcriptions on short notice and with tight deadlines, which was helpful in keeping the project on schedule due to my time constraints. And thanks to my business partner, Ed Jones, who covered for me at many meetings and on many projects while I was working on the book.

My sincere thanks to all of you.

CHAPTER 1

Characteristics of Micro Cap

This chapter will attempt to answer the following questions:

- What is a micro cap stock?
- Why do they exist?

THE NEBULOUS MICRO CAP (WHAT IS A MICRO CAP STOCK?)

Investors often refer to "the market" when speaking about stocks as a group. However, knowledgeable investors will agree that not all stocks are created equal. Different investors will often focus on more narrowly defined segments of the market. When looking at the composition of the market as a whole, these investors will normally classify stocks by certain characteristics. The two most fundamental characteristics of classification within the investment community are those of value and of growth stocks. Most investors are familiar with the concepts of growth and value investing, although agreeing on the definition of either is often a topic of debate among informed observers.

Taken further, the growth and value styles can be divided into subgroups that categorize the investments by market capitalization. For example, there is large cap growth and mid cap value. These capitalization ranges are typically broken down into large cap, mid cap, and small cap when referring to the size of the underlying companies. These style and market cap definitions are the most basic categories of classification when referring to investment managers and the stocks they own. But when dividing the market of stocks by capitalization, a very large number of small public companies virtually disappear from the investor radar screen. These are a segment of companies often referred to as *micro caps*. It should be no surprise that, like the definitions of value and growth, the threshold sizes for large, mid, and small capitalization stocks are also subject to debate.

The market capitalization of a company is arrived at by multiplying the number of outstanding shares of common stock in that company by its current market price per share to arrive at the total value of all shares outstanding.

$$\text{Market capitalization} = (\text{shares outstanding} \times \text{current market price per share})$$

To some degree, the demarcation of market capitalization is influenced by the many widely published market indexes such as the Standard & Poor's (S&P) 500 or the Dow Jones Industrial Average. The threshold sizes for market segmentation are often related in some ways to the relative market capitalization of the stocks contained within a popular market index.

For example, the S&P 500 Index is considered to be a large capitalization index. The smallest stock in the index has a market cap of $414 million, with the largest having a market cap of $286.6 billion. The 500 stocks that constitute the index have an average market capitalization of $17.9 billion. The index has a median market cap of $7.5 billion as of June 30, 2004. (June 30, 2004 is the date of all market capitalization data throughout this book unless otherwise noted.) These types of statistics will lead market participants to general ranges that define the boundaries of market capitalization segments. Currently, most market participants agree that large capitalization stocks are those that have a market capitalization of outstanding shares in excess of $5.0 billion.

Another way to approach the issue of defining market capitalization boundaries is to study the market cap distribution of all public companies. Using a standard distribution of market capitalization values, the market cap of all public companies can be divided into groups based on the range of market capitalization in which they appear. The Center for Research in Securities Prices (CRSP) at the University of Chicago maintains an extensive database of stock prices often used for this type of market cap research. The CRSP produces a database of market performance indexes that are broken down by market value. The index that represents the smallest 20 percent of publicly traded common stocks is typically used as a proxy for the micro cap market. CRSP ranks the top 20 percent of the market in terms of capitalization as large cap, the next 30 percent of market capitalization following that as mid cap, the following 30 percent is a proxy for small cap, and as mentioned, the smallest 20 percent is considered micro cap. In addition, there have been those who segment the top 10 percent of companies by market cap and consider them to be mega cap companies. Conversely, the quantitative research group at Merrill Lynch, led by Richard Bernstein, has dubbed stocks with a market cap of less than $100 million the "nano cap" sector.

The many academic studies of market cap segmentation coupled with the growth in the investment consulting profession have resulted in the definitions of capital markets becoming more structured. Institutional investors now segment the investment markets into narrow sectors ranging from nano caps through mega caps. This segmentation of the public investable market has given rise in part to the micro cap asset class.

As mentioned, there have been a large number of academic studies that explore the market cap segmentation of public companies. The outgrowth of one such study was the Russell 2000 Index, published by Frank Russell Company, of Tacoma, Washington. Each year, this company reshuffles the universe of U.S.-domiciled companies by total market value and selects the 3,000 largest U.S. domestic public companies. They then create the Russell 2000 from the bottom two-thirds of the 3,000 largest companies. The new universe contains stocks with share prices greater than $1 that are publicly traded as of May 30 of each year.

In addition, Russell must receive documentation from each company that includes a company description and confirms the number of shares outstanding in order for the company to be eligible for inclusion. The Russell 2000 Index has become the most popular small cap benchmark against which the performance of small cap portfolio managers is measured.

With the introduction of the Frank Russell Company Russell 2000 Index, small cap stocks finally had an index of their own. The Russell 2000 was introduced in 1985, and by the early 1990s there was a proliferation of small cap mutual funds benchmarked against the index. The Russell 2000 is now the most widely quoted index of U.S. small cap stocks. Prior to the creation of the Russell 2000, micro caps were often grouped with small cap stocks. In addition, as mentioned earlier, the boundaries of where micro cap stocks ended and small cap stocks started were often debated within the financial community.

It was not until the early 1990s that micro cap stocks began to develop their own identity and their characteristics evolved sufficiently to separate them from the small cap segment. This was in part the result of the large and growing number of micro cap stocks in the public arena. It was also due in part to the continued refinement of market segmentation within the professional consulting and investment community.

Currently, the Russell 2000 has a range of market caps that has fallen for three years in a row, as of the most recent rebalancing on June 30, 2003. The largest stock in the index has a market cap of $1.2 billion, whereas the smallest stock has a market cap of $117 million. In comparison, the range in 2002 was $1.31 billion down to $131 million. The rebalancing pushes the weighted-average market cap down to about $646.9 million versus $696.6 million when the index was rebalanced in 2002. The average market cap for stocks in the newly rebalanced index is $443 million, while the median capitalization is $350 million. This index clearly reflects the definition of small cap within the investment community. Currently, most market participants agree that small capitalization stocks are considered those in the range of $500 million to $1.5 billion. Thus, if large cap is $5.0 billion and up and small cap is $500 million to $1.5 billion, then by elimination mid cap stocks are those that fall in the $1.5 billion to $5.0 billion ranges. This still leaves the definition of micro cap as an unanswered question.

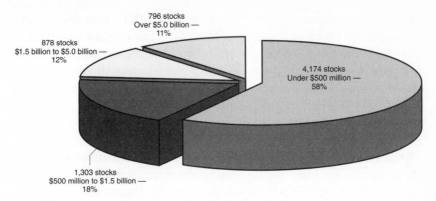

FIGURE 1.1 Distribution of reporting public companies by market capitalization, June 30, 2004.

These commonly accepted descriptions of market capitalization leave out one very large segment of the public markets. Currently there are more than 4,000 stocks listed on the New York and American stock exchanges, and the Nasdaq and over-the-counter (OTC) markets that have a market capitalization of less than $500 million. Some observers might argue that micro caps begin at below $400 million, or even below $300 million, but in any case the absolute number of these micro cap companies is large. For purposes of this analysis, a market cap of below $500 million will be considered a micro cap. Wherever the line is drawn, these small company stocks are generally known among professional investors as micro caps. In absolute number, the micro cap universe of 4,000 stocks has roughly twice the number of stocks than the universe of companies with market capitalization of over $500 million! (See Figure 1.1.)

THE MICRO CAP DILEMMA (WHY DO THEY EXIST?)

In the world of professional investing, micro cap stocks are often overlooked simply because of their small size. To a large degree, this is the result of the growing size and scale of professional investment management. For example, small cap investment managers who offer a good performance track record often find themselves with a billion dollars or more of investment capital to manage on behalf of their clients. A simple search of the Morningstar universe of small cap mutual funds yields over 1,450 small cap funds with an aggregate of over $900 billion under management in these funds alone. It does not consider the separate private accounts of these institutional money managers. In addition, it does not consider the hundreds of private institutional money managers who don't manage a public mutual fund.

In the Plan Sponsor Network (PSN) database of money managers published by Thomson Financial, there are over 1,900 small cap managers listed with an estimated $850 billion of small cap assets under management. This creates a situation where, for the purposes of liquidity and efficiency, professional investors must focus on small company opportunities that provide the scale and liquidity required to invest these larger pools of funds.

Professional investors also have limited resources available in terms of research capabilities to analyze and screen the thousands of smaller companies. In many instances, they rely on Wall Street research analysts to provide basic coverage of small company opportunities. However, Wall Street research is often hesitant to focus on small companies if those small companies don't appear to provide investment banking opportunities for the research firm or if the companies don't have sufficient market liquidity to allow for easy trading in the stock by larger institutions. This creates a situation where many small high-quality companies that are not seeking additional investment capital or have limited trading volume go largely uncovered by Wall Street firms and are largely unnoticed by small cap portfolio managers.

The world of small cap stocks is also where many research analysts begin their careers in the investment business. This is not to say that all analysts covering small cap stocks are new or inexperienced; however, a large number of analysts often begin their career paths in the small cap arena. This new analyst phenomenon often leads to research that is of lower quality than the research published by more seasoned analysts who are focused on the mid cap and large cap investment arena. From a business perspective, it makes sense that the resources of better, more experienced analysts are allocated to opportunities of the size and scale that are more meaningful to large institutional investors. Large companies tend to be more complex, too. In addition, these larger companies often provide more active investment banking opportunities for the sell-side brokerage firm as well. So it's easy to see why many small and micro cap companies are either undercovered or not covered at all by Wall Street research firms.

In addition to these burdens, small and micro cap companies are often considered riskier by institutional investors. This notion of high risk may run contrary to the professional investors' fiduciary duty, which is often prescribed as limiting risk in the context of their portfolio management. So in the face of fiduciary responsibility, a typical professional investor would feel more comfortable owning Anheuser-Busch, with a market capitalization of $42.6 billion, than Samuel Adams, the small microbrewery based in Boston, Massachusetts, with a market capitalization of $217.0 million. Without regard to the idea that the smaller brewery is growing at a much faster rate (and makes better beer, in this writer's opinion) and also carries a generally lower valuation than Anheuser-Busch, professional investors, because of their fiduciary obligations and their perception of risk, would likely own Anheuser-Busch over Sam Adams.

When considering an investment, many institutional and professional investors equate a low share price with low quality or high risk. A share price of below $5, or even below $1, often brings to mind the notion of "penny stocks" with professional investors. Penny stocks are generally low-priced stocks normally trading below $5 and often trading at below $1 per share. They are speculative securities of very small companies. By definition, all penny stocks trade in the OTC Bulletin Board (OTCBB) or the pink sheets, but do not trade on national exchanges such as the New York Stock Exchange or the Nasdaq Stock Market.

The OTCBB is an electronic quotation system that displays real-time quotes, last-sale prices, and volume information for many OTC securities that are not listed on the Nasdaq Stock Market or a national securities exchange. Brokerage firms subscribe to the system and can use the OTCBB to look up prices or enter quotes for OTC securities. Although the National Association of Securities Dealers (NASD) oversees the OTCBB, the OTCBB is not part of the Nasdaq Stock Market. Unscrupulous stockbrokers will often claim that an OTCBB company is a Nasdaq company to mislead investors into thinking that a company is really bigger than it is.

The pink sheets are named for the color of paper on which these stock quotes are printed. They are listings of price quotes for companies that trade on the over-the-counter (OTC) market. OTC market makers are the brokers who commit to buying and selling the securities of OTC issuers. They use the pink sheets to publish bid and ask prices for companies of which they may want to buy and sell shares. A company named Pink Sheets LLC, formerly known as the National Quotation Bureau, publishes the pink sheets in both hard copy and electronic format. Pink Sheets LLC is not registered with the Securities and Exchange Commission as a stock exchange, nor does the SEC regulate its activities. The structure and use of penny stock issues is discussed in more detail in Chapter **12.**

It is important to understand that the share price of a stock has no bearing on or relationship to market cap. A perfect example of this is Nortel Networks, with a share price of $2.70 as of June 30, 2003. Nortel is not a micro cap stock or a penny stock. With 3.85 billion (yes, billion!) shares outstanding, Nortel sports a market cap of $10.4 billion ($2.70 share price × 3.85 billion shares outstanding = $10.4 billion market cap). Nortel Networks is a large cap stock. (See Figure 1.2.) Conversely, Seaboard is an agribusiness company listed on the American Stock Exchange that currently trades at $207 per share. With 1.255 million shares outstanding, the company has a market cap of $260 million ($207 share price × 1.255 million shares = $260 million market cap). With a share price of $207 per share, this is a micro cap stock. Thus, small companies can have big share prices and big companies can have small share prices. Share price in general is has no direct relation to the size of a company.

In fact, share price has no relationship to the size of a business. Consider the Internet boom for a moment. There were many multi-billion-dollar market cap companies that had no revenues, few employees, and limited tangible assets. In many ways, market cap reflects the consensus of investor opinion about the future prospects for a company.

The classic case study of this phenomenon is that of Amazon

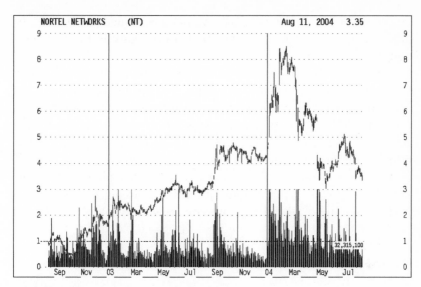

FIGURE 1.2 Nortel Networks price chart.

.com and Barnes & Noble. In May 1997, Amazon went public with a market cap of about $400 million. By January 1999, the share price had reached about $100 and the market cap was $38 billion, as compared to Barnes & Noble, the nation's largest bookseller, with a market cap at the time of around $2.6 billion. In 1998, Barnes & Noble had revenues of $3 billion and earnings of $1.29 per share, while Amazon had revenues of $610 million and lost $.42 per share. Yet with sales one-fourth those of Barnes & Noble, and considering that it was losing money versus turning a profit of $1.29 per share, Amazon commanded a market value 14 times that of Barnes & Noble. And Amazon started out as a micro cap opportunity. (See Figure 1.3.)

Amazon is now widely held in institutional investment portfolios. At the time of its initial public offering (IPO), it is unlikely that many institutional investors owned the company. The belief was that individual investors were primarily willing to support early-stage industries such as computer companies and the Internet. This was the main driver behind micro cap stocks. However, few institutional investors would consider micro cap issues as viable investments because, in many instances, the business

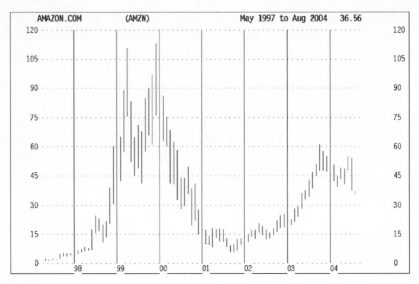

FIGURE 1.3   Amazon.com price chart.

models and technologies were largely unproven. It was only when the companies became large enough that institutional investors would consider the possibility of investing in them.

Each year hundreds of these small, undiscovered companies grow to become hot small cap opportunities as they emerge from the micro cap universe. When these small companies reach $500 million to $700 million dollars in market capitalization, they typically become the focus of small cap research analysts and small cap investment management companies that are actively seeking emerging opportunities from the micro cap segment. This leaves thousands of stocks to go virtually unnoticed by the professional investment community until they graduate into the ranks of the small cap and beyond.

In the year ended June 30, 2004, 554 companies graduated from the micro cap to the small cap arena simply due to price appreciation. In fact, the average 12-month return of the graduating class was 113 percent. During that same year, 651 companies descended from the ranks above micro cap into the micro cap arena when their market capitalization shrank to below $500 million.

At the end of March 2003, American Airlines had a market capitalization of around $300 million. As of June 30, 2004, the stock closed at $12. American Airlines existed as a micro cap because of a change in the dynamics of the airline industry as a result of the attack of September 11, 2001. Just as the consensus of investor opinion reflected a positive outlook for Amazon, a similar consensus of investor opinion had a very negative outlook for American Airlines. It is these very extremes in investor emotion that often create opportunity. And it is these extremes that are often reflected at some point within the micro cap segment. However, to better understand these extremes, an investor must understand the information advantage. Chapter 2 will examine the concept of the information advantage.

The Information Advantage

This chapter will attempt to answer the following questions:

- Is there a possible information advantage for diligent micro cap investors?
- How can this information advantage be explained in the context of efficient market theory?

UNDERSTANDING THE INFORMATION ADVANTAGE: EFFICIENT MARKET THEORY

The information advantage is the reason that opportunity exists within the micro cap arena. However, an understanding of the concept of the efficient market theory (EMT) is required to understand the information advantage. Efficient capital markets and the efficient capital market group of theories have important implications for micro cap investors as well as for security valuation. The definition of an efficient capital market is relatively simple. However, it is less frequently asked why capital markets should be efficient.

The basis for EMT is premised on certain conditions that market participants assume exist when examining capital market

opportunities. The first premise of an efficient market is that
there are a large number of profit-maximizing investors concerned with the analysis of information related to the investment
opportunities within a market. And it is further assumed that
these participants operate relatively independently of one
another. A second assumption about efficient markets is that new
information about securities arrives to the market in a random
fashion. In addition, the announcement of this information is generally independent of other new announcements over time. The
third assumption of an efficient market is particularly important
in the micro cap arena. This condition assumes investors will
adjust the market price of securities quickly to reflect the perceived effect of new information in the market. But it is generally
agreed that at times when price adjustments are reflected in the
market, they are not always perfect. It is not unusual to see over-
reactions or underreactions to new market information. Markets
can be very emotional over the short run. But it is often difficult
to anticipate and identify these market reactions.

The idea that the market attempts to adjust securities prices
quickly is based on the first premise that there are a large number
of profit-maximizing investors attempting to reflect that information in the value of a stock price. When the effects of random
information coming to the market in an independent fashion are
coupled with the presumed large number of investors adjusting
stock prices rapidly to reflect new information, it is assumed that
price changes are independent and random.

Therefore, the crucial point of the efficient market discussion
is that the adjustment process requires a large number of investors who follow the stock and analyze the impact of new
information on the stock. That group of investors then buys or
sells the stock to adjust the price to reflect the new information
available in the market. It is at this point in the theory where a
potential information advantage begins to develop within the
micro cap sector. The general academic conclusion about efficient markets is that securities prices at any particular point in
time will reflect an unbiased outlook of all currently available
information in the market. So an efficient market is one in which
securities prices adjust rapidly to the delivery of new information
and current stock prices fully reflect all available information
including the future risk involved in the security price.

The early analysis of the efficient market concept was often called the *random walk hypothesis*. A pivotal study that attempted to organize a large amount of information about the random walk theory was done by Eugene Fama in a *Journal of Finance* article entitled "Efficient Capital Markets: A Review of Theory and Empirical Work," which was published in May 1970. Fama's article presented the efficient market theory in terms of a fair game model.

Unlike work done under the random walk hypothesis, the fair game model deals with price at a specified period. It assumes that the price of a security fully reflects all available information at that period. The model requires that the price formation process be specified in enough detail so it is possible to indicate what is meant by "fully reflected." Fama's analysis went on to divide the efficient market hypothesis and empirical tests into three categories depending on the information set involved. His theory said that EMT comes in various strengths, depending on what information is, by theory, assumed to be reflected in the stock price.

Weak-Form Efficient Market Theory

The weak-form EMT maintains that all information about past market prices is already reflected in the stock price. The weak form assumes not only that current stock prices fully reflect all stock market information but that they include the historical sequence of prices, price changes, trading volume, and any other market-related information that is publicly available. Because current price should reflect all past price changes and any other stock market information, this hypothesis implies that there should be no relationship between past price changes and future price changes. Thus, the famous disclaimer: "Past performance is no indication of future results." The theory concludes that any analysis that depends on past price changes or past market data to predict future price changes or future market data should have little value in terms of investment contribution. The implication of this is that all of the rules of charting and technical analysis, which focus on past price and volume changes, are entirely useless. This is the conclusion in spite of the fact that many large Wall Street firms employ one or more full-time technical analysts on their staff.

Semi-Strong-Form Efficient Market Theory

The semi-strong-form EMT maintains that all publicly available information about a company is already reflected in its stock price. It asserts that securities prices adjust rapidly to reflect the release of all new public information. The semi-strong hypothesis includes the weak-form hypothesis because all public information, including all market information such as stock prices and trading volume and all nonmarket information such as earnings and stock splits, would be fully reflected in share values. The direct implication of the semi-strong hypothesis is that investors who act on important new information after it is public cannot obtain market-beating profits from the transaction. In theory this is because the security price already reflects the effect of the new public information. A consequence of this version of EMT is that the analysis of earnings, corporate filings, press releases, interest rate changes, and other fundamental data analysis are essentially useless. This should give cause to the elimination of stock research that is earnings focused.

Strong-Form Efficient Market Theory

The strong-form EMT maintains that stock prices fully reflect all information, both public and private. It implies that no group of investors has access to information relative to the formation of prices that would be of advantage to them over other investors. Therefore, no group of investors should be able to consistently derive above-average profits from the market. The strong-form hypothesis includes both the weak and the semi-strong forms. The strong form requires not only efficient markets where prices adjust rapidly to the release of new information, but it also requires perfect information markets where all information is available to everyone at the same time. This form of the efficient market theory contends that because all information is immediately available to everyone and rapidly discounted by everyone, no group has meaningful access to important new information and therefore nobody can derive above-market profits over long periods of time. The implication of this form of EMT is that industry analysis and even inside information are useless.

It was probably the strong-form EMT that gave rise to the old joke about the two efficient market theorists that is told in every graduate business school capital markets class. It goes like this: There are two efficient market theorists walking down the street, when they see a $100 bill on the ground. Looking at each other, they precede to walk right by it, neither making any effort to pick up the cash. Why? Because as efficient market theorists, they conclude that if the $100 bill were real, it would have been picked up already.

The Random Walk Theory

There is another flavor of the EMT, known as the random walk theory. This concept was first put forward by Burton Malkiel in his book *A Random Walk Down Wall Street* (New York: W.W. Norton, 1990), in which he challenges the idea that stock prices can be predicted. He essentially concludes that no market strategy can consistently outperform a buy-and-hold index approach.

The basic principle of the random walk is that there is no such thing as a free lunch. The opportunity to get something for nothing is not available to investors. The $100 bill that the EMTs walked by would never be lying there. This is because the stock market is a very efficient mechanism in the long run. It reflects an ongoing battle among many intelligent active investors who provide strong competition to any and all market participants. Competition ensures that there are no quick and easy profits and that outsmarting the market is exceedingly difficult. Other participants in the market are just as sharp and aggressive, and they are not about to allow someone else to make a profit if they can make it themselves.

The result of this competition inside the stock market ensures that transactions take place at a competitive price and that those prices reflect a clearing level that both the buyer and the seller deem reasonable. Said another way, the buyers buy because as buyers they believe the stock is undervalued or, at worst, fairly priced. In theory, once the buyers become the owners, they would never sell a stock if they believed the stock was too cheap or undervalued. Sellers, however, would sell a stock that they considered overpriced to buyers who believed they were getting a bargain. And on average, you could say that both the buyers and the sellers were equally correct. Their competitive positions result in a general standoff with the vast majority of stock market transactions taking place at what the broad consensus of thousands of shareholders would consider fair prices. The competition between millions of active buyers and sellers, with all investors trying to make a return on their investment that is higher than that of the market, suggests that stock prices fairly reflect the future returns from holding a particular stock. This, Malkiel concludes, suggests there is no way to tell which stock will provide superior returns that has not already been imagined by other investors. Thus, there is no way to predict which stock will go up and which stock will go down on any particular day. The theory would hold that one stock has just as good a chance as any other stock.

But stock prices do change on a daily basis. Some prices are up each day, while others are down. Because competition in the marketplace implies that investors cannot anticipate these changes, the changes must essentially be random. It is as if someone were flipping a coin in an attempt to decide whether a stock price will go up or down. And tomorrow the coin is flipped again, and the following day it is flipped again. As a result, stock prices wander up and down randomly in irregular and unpredictable patterns in a manner that is typically called a "random walk."

Efficient market theorists of all disciplines would conclude that beating the market over a long period of time is not possible. The weak-form EMT suggests that technical analysis or price pattern observations cannot work. The semi-strong EMT eliminates the possibility that fundamental analysis can help an investor outperform the market. And the strong-form EMT concludes that even material inside information will not provide an advantage over the long term. The random walk theory concludes that the continuing battle between buyers and sellers precludes anyone from picking stocks as a group that will outperform an index. Index-like performance is the best an investor can hope to achieve in terms of investment performance, according to the efficient market theorist. And the most efficient way to achieve that performance is to invest in index funds or index shares.

The Practical Answer

A review of the academic literature will show that there are various research studies that both support and call into question each segment of the EMT as put forth by Fama. There is a similar group of studies that question numerous aspects of the random walk theory as put forth by Malkiel. More important to this discussion is the fact that there is a small but growing body of academic research suggesting that some aspects of the efficient market theory can be questioned when looking at smaller and very small stocks.

At this point, a rigorous review and analysis of the mathematical foundation of each form of the efficient market theory might help show the weakness in EMT. However, for the purposes of this book it is more meaningful to ask some straightforward questions about the general concept of the efficient market theory and examine the probable answers to those questions. The questions are simple:

- Why do some actively managed funds beat the market over long periods of time?
- Why, at times, do whole companies sell for less than the market value of the net cash on the balance sheet?
- Why do small capitalization stocks outperform large capitalization stocks over time?
- Why have stock prices generally gone up over time?
- Why do most micro cap managers outperform their benchmarks?

In an interesting analysis in the *Journal of Financial Management* ("A Cross Sectional Approach to Market Liquidity," May 1982), Frank Riley suggests that the market can be divided into three different tiers. The top tier contains companies large enough to accommodate all institutional investors who wish to take a meaningful position and retain liquidity. A middle tier consists of companies that are large enough to be acquired by most institutional investors and large investors, although they are probably too small to be of interest to the top 100 institutional investors. And then there is a bottom tier of companies that are not large enough to be considered by most institutional investors. The study estimates that the total number of public companies in this bottom tier at any given time is between 5,000 and 8,000. Riley concludes that analysts should be encouraged to concentrate their efforts on middle-tier firms because these stocks contain the characteristics to ascend to the top tier of the market, but they do not receive the attention given to top-tier stocks. So the market may not be as efficient in reflecting all the information about these middle-tier stocks.

Riley concludes that if there is a difference in the number of analysts following a stock, one could conceivably argue a difference in efficiency of the information reflected in the stock's value. In the case of a top-tier stock, all new information regarding the stock would be well publicized and numerous analysts would evaluate the effect. News about middle-tier firms is not as well publicized, and fewer analysts following these firms would be reflecting their opinions about the impact of the news. Thus, prices may not adjust as rapidly to new information, and therefore concentrating on those middle-tier stocks could conceivably add value over long periods of time. After the Riley study, a number of additional studies came out that indicate superior return profiles for stocks that are followed by fewer analysts. As discussed in Chapter 1, most micro cap stocks have few if any analysts following them. Furthermore, the quality of the analysis is often lower than that of the analysis on larger capitalization securities.

It's fair to conclude that information concerning larger stocks, which are more widely held by institutional investors, would more rapidly reflect changes in information available about the securities due to the high levels of scrutiny and analysis that are focused on those securities. It is unlikely that there is any information, public or private, that an individual investor can discern about a giant company, such as Microsoft, that the institutions and legions of analysts who cover Microsoft don't already know.

Conversely, it would then be safe to assume that securities with little or no coverage by institutional investors and a low percentage of institutional ownership would require a longer period of time for all publicly available information to be fully reflected in the share price. It seems possible that a diligent individual or institutional investor could discover some level of pertinent information not reflected in the share price of a small company that is not adequately researched by investment analysts and institutions.

VENTURE CAPITAL THEORY

No single theory of market performance seems to address all the issues with regard to the efficient market theory; however, it is generally agreed that over long periods of time the markets tend to reflect all available information and are relatively efficient in the reflection of that information in terms of securities value. It is also agreed that over shorter periods of time this information may not be fully reflected in the market valuation of common stocks or that markets may overreact to information. It is that short-term relative inefficiency that allows for a potential information advantage to the micro cap investor.

There are some simple statistical data that might further support the idea that there is an information advantage available to micro cap investors. First, it is known that over long periods of time, stock market prices tend to go higher in the aggregate to reflect the economic growth in the underlying economy. Second, we also know that smaller capitalization stocks provide larger returns than big capitalization stocks over those same long periods of time. From these two simple facts, when considered within the framework of the efficient market theory, it would be possible to conclude that smaller stocks are less efficient in reflecting all available information in the market, and although they reflect that information over time, managers of small and micro capitalization stock indexes have the opportunity to use that information advantage in producing higher returns.

As stocks become larger and are more widely held by institutions and more fully studied by investors, it becomes increasingly difficult to gain a similar information advantage. Large capitalization stock prices, in theory, will react more quickly to available market information, therefore making it more difficult to capitalize on the information advantage. Discovering and capturing this information advantage is the key to achieving investment performance in the micro cap arena.

No single market theory alone explains the unique investment characteristics of the micro cap sector. The empirical data suggest that the micro cap sector is less efficient in the short term than larger capitalization sectors of the market. As we have discussed, there are a number of market theories that may help to partly explain this phenomenon, but no single "unified theory" exists. However, when certain elements of venture capital theory are added to the existing data, a more unified theory that could reasonably explain the information advantage emerges.

The Public-Private Bridge

There is a large body of academic literature on the principal agent problem in private venture capital transactions. This literature focuses on the conflict of interest between an agent who is an entrepreneur needing financing and a principal who is the investor providing the funds for the venture. The theory has identified a number of ways in which the investor or principal can mitigate these conflicts. First, the investor can engage in information collection before deciding whether to invest, in order to screen out unprofitable projects or bad entrepreneurs. Second, the investor can engage in information collection and monitoring once the project is under way. Third, the allocation of cash flow between the entrepreneur and the investor can be designed to provide incentives for the entrepreneur to behave profitably. In these three approaches, we can find a series of information advantage opportunities that may also be found in the micro cap arena.

In the first instance, when investors engage in information collection before deciding whether to invest, in order to screen out unprofitable projects or bad entrepreneurs, a uniform opinion of a company often emerges. In the micro cap arena, a review of a company might find an incompetent management team. Or it might find a company that has an outdated and inferior product or service. This uniform opinion can become the "conventional wisdom" about the company, and the company is often relegated to the ranks of the walking dead among the micro cap universe. Larger shareholders in a micro cap company faced with such a reputation have a very limited range of potential buyers for their shares.

In many ways, the agent of venture capital theory and the selling shareholder of the micro cap company are similar. In each case, they have a relatively narrow universe of potential buyers, and these potential buyers are engaged in information collection in an attempt to screen out bad companies or bad management. The real distinction is that the micro cap seller can estimate by the current trading price the approximate price that a buyer might be likely to pay, and the seller rather than the company will receive the proceeds of the sale. The buyer, being one of only a few, can often extract a significant discount from the seller, much like the venture capital principal agent model.

In the second venture capital instance, the investor can engage in information collection and monitoring once the project is under way. This is likewise true of the micro cap company. In the instance of the venture capital relationship, the availability of additional capital might be predicated on reaching certain milestones. The same is true of micro cap investing. A micro cap company might announce some changes to its business or strategy. This might create some additional investor interest in the company but not cause any meaningful change in the value of the traded shares. After the company achieves certain results, interested investors might then begin to actively buy shares in the company. Micro cap portfolio managers are often monitoring the results of a select list of companies in anticipation of a certain milestone before they are willing to buy the company stock. Again, this is very similar to the monitoring in which a venture capital investor might engage prior to making a financial commitment or providing additional capital to a company. The principal difference in this second transaction is who receives the investment: an existing micro cap shareholder who is selling shares or the company. Large selling shareholders may sense a liquidity opportunity that was otherwise absent. Buyers sense an emerging opportunity at a reasonable valuation.

In the third venture capital instance, where the allocation of cash flow between the entrepreneur and the investor can be designed to provide incentives for the entrepreneur to behave profitably, there is also a similar model within the micro cap arena. In the micro cap world, shareholder activism is a daily event. In fact, later in this book we will discuss how to identify micro cap opportunities by studying who is taking a significant stake within a company. Like the venture capital model, the activist shareholder model in the micro cap arena seeks to align the interests of management and its shareholders. The performance is set by agreement prior to the investment. In the case of the micro cap investor, a large stake in the company is usually acquired first, and then financial and legal pressure is brought to bear on management. This is often done by a small group of large shareholders with the explicit message that things will change or management will change. In most instances, the management sees the light and behaves in a way that is mutually beneficial to them and the shareholders, just as in the venture capital model.

CONCLUSION

Micro cap stocks have some unique characteristics that are a result of their size. Like their larger capitalization publicly traded cousins, micro caps live within the boundaries of efficient market theory but behave slightly differently than their larger cousins. When compared to larger cap stocks, micro caps do not seem to reflect all available information as efficiently as larger cap public companies. This results in higher expected returns and higher volatility than with large stocks. But the higher returns more than compensate for the added volatility. This leads us to the theory that there can be an information advantage available to diligent micro cap investors because the micro cap sector is less efficient in the speed at which it reflects information. If this were true, EMT would be called into question.

But when comparing the micro cap investment sector to venture capital investing, the EMT inconsistencies within micro caps can be reconciled when considered in light of the principal agent venture capital model. This suggests that micro caps are a sector unto themselves. The sector has many of the elements of larger capitalization stocks as well as many characteristics of venture capital investments. In many ways, the micro cap sector is a bridge between the public equity markets and the private venture capital markets and displays the unified characteristics of both. Chapter 3 will discuss these unified characteristics in more detail.

Micro Cap Stocks as an Asset Class

This chapter will attempt to answer the following questions:

- Are micro cap investors adequately rewarded for the risk undertaken?
- Are micro caps similar to venture capital?

INVESTMENT PERFORMANCE: SMALL VERSUS LARGE STOCKS

Among all the academic literature about finance and investing, some of the most well-known and often-cited studies are those that concern the performance of small company stocks. Even the most inexperienced investor seems to understand that smaller capitalization stocks outperform larger stocks over the long term. In addition, most investors seem to understand that the performance of smaller stocks also carries a higher risk or more volatility than that of their larger cousins. Even though investors realize that small stocks outperform large stocks over the long run, they don't seem to understand that this performance is achieved within significant cycles of underperformance and outperformance relative to bigger stocks. It is the very instability of this relationship between the performance of large and small stocks

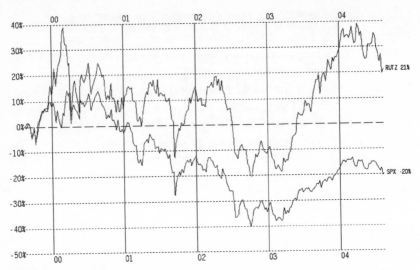

FIGURE 3.1 Russell 2000 versus S&P 500, August 20, 1999 to August 11, 2004.

that creates the investment value of small and micro cap stocks in a multiasset class portfolio.

As shown in Figure 3.1, the relative performance of small stocks, as represented by the Russell 2000 Index, versus larger stocks, as represented by the S&P 500 Index, is superior over long periods of time. A number of important academic works regarding small cap stocks began to show that smaller capitalization stocks had historically provided superior returns over and above what could be explained by the capital asset pricing model. It appeared that even when adjusting for the higher risk of smaller cap stocks, they provided superior returns.

To understand this phenomenon, it is worthwhile to make a brief survey of the key constructs of the capital asset pricing model (CAPM) and related market theory, as well as how they evolved over time. Readers who are familiar with capital asset pricing and market theory may want to skip over this section.

A SURVEY OF MODERN PORTFOLIO THEORY

Any discussion related to the history of the theory of stock price behavior generally starts with Harry Markowitz. In his pioneering book *Portfolio Selection: Efficient Diversification of Investment* (John Wiley & Sons, 1959), Markowitz sets forth some ground-breaking work based on earlier academic studies he had published. The Markowitz model is a single-period model, in which an investor forms a portfolio at the start of a given period. The investor's objective is to maximize the portfolio's expected return, subject to an acceptable level of risk. Said differently, the investor seeks to minimize risk, subject to an acceptable expected rate of return. The assumption of a single time period in conjunction with assumptions about the investor's attitude toward risk allows risk to be defined by the variance or standard deviation of the portfolio's return.

As additional securities are added to a portfolio, the expected return and standard deviation change in very specific ways, based on how the newly added securities co-vary with the other securities in the portfolio. The best that an investor can do in theory is defined by a curved frontier that is the upper half of a hyperbola, as shown in Figure 3.2. The curve is known as the *efficient frontier.* According to Markowitz, investors select portfolios along this curve, according to their tolerance for risk. An investor who can live with a lot of risk might select portfolio 1. A more risk-averse investor would accept a lower return for correspondingly

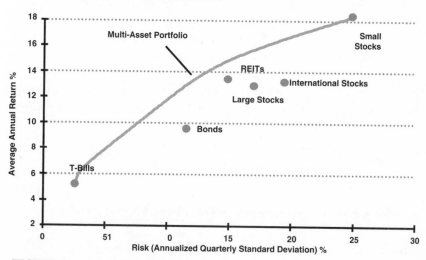

FIGURE 3.2 The efficient frontier.

lower risk and likely choose portfolio 2. One of the major insights of the Markowitz model is that a security's expected return, coupled with how it co-varies with other securities, determines how it is added to an investor portfolio.

Using the Markowitz framework, William Sharpe, along with John Lintner and Jan Mossin independently of one another, developed the theoretical constructs for what is known as the *capital asset pricing model* (CAPM). The CAPM assumes that investors use the basic logic of Markowitz in forming portfolios. It further assumes that there is a risk-free asset that has a certain return. With a risk-free asset, the efficient frontier in Figure 3.2 is no longer the best that investors can do. The straight line in Figure 3.3 has the risk-free rate as its intercept. It is tangent to the efficient frontier and represents the boundary of the investment opportunity set. Investors choose portfolios along the capital market line, which shows combinations of the risk-free asset and the risky portfolio M. In order for markets to be in equilibrium (quantity supplied = quantity demanded), portfolio M must be the market portfolio of all risky assets. So all investors combine the market portfolio and the risk-free asset, and the only risk

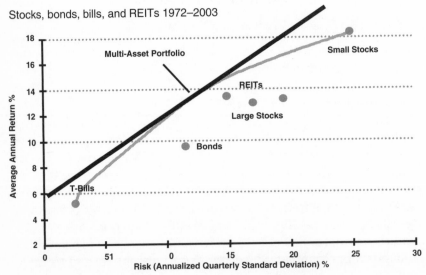

FIGURE 3.3 The efficient frontier with opportunity boundary.

or premium that investors are paid for bearing is the risk associated with the market portfolio.

From the CAPM emerges the concept of *beta*. The beta coefficient is the measure of risk as it relates to the broader market. So beta represents the portion of an asset's risk that cannot be diversified away. This is the risk that investors are compensated for bearing. The CAPM equation says that the expected return of any risky asset is a linear function of its tendency to co-vary with the market portfolio. So if the CAPM is an accurate description of the way assets are priced, this positive linear relation should be observed when average portfolio returns are compared to portfolio betas. Said differently, the higher the beta of a portfolio, the higher its return should be. Further, when beta is included as an explanatory variable, in theory no other variable should be able to explain cross-sectional differences in average returns. Beta should be all that matters in the CAPM.

The CAPM is a simple model based on simple financial reasoning. It certainly does not capture the dynamics of the broad market, but rather tries to explain a central market mechanism. However, some of the assumptions that underlie the basic model are not realistic. As a result, a number of permutations and extensions of the basic CAPM have been proposed that relax one or more of the CAPM assumptions. Instead of simply extending an existing theory, Stephen Ross, another academic, addresses this concern by developing a completely unrelated model known as the *arbitrage pricing theory* (APT). Unlike the CAPM, which is a model of financial markets at equilibrium, the APT starts with the premise that arbitrage opportunities should not be present in efficient financial markets. This assumption is less restrictive than those required to derive the CAPM.

The APT begins with the assumption that there are n number of factors that cause asset returns to systematically deviate from their expected values. The theory does not identify the factors or specify how large the number n is. It simply reasons that these n factors cause returns to vary together. There may be other, firm-specific, reasons for returns to differ from their expected values, but these firm-specific deviations are not related across all companies or stocks. Since the firm-specific deviations are not at all related to one another, all return variations not related to the n common factors could be diversified away. Ross concludes that in order to prevent arbitrage, an asset's expected return must be a linear function of its sensitivity to the n common factors. As with the CAPM, Ross created an expression for expected return that is a linear function of the asset's sensitivity to systematic or market risk. Under the assumptions of APT, there are n numbers of sources of systematic risk, whereas there is only one in a CAPM world. The conclusion is that many factors impact market returns, and many factors impact stock returns.

The theoretical flaw in both the CAPM and the APT is the fact that they are static, or single-period, models. They ignore the real-life fact that capital markets are multiperiod in nature. Robert Merton's *intertemporal capital asset pricing model* (ICAPM) attempts to capture this multiperiod aspect of financial market equilibrium. The ICAPM framework recognizes that the investment opportunities might shift over time, and investors would like to hedge their investments against unfavorable shifts in the set of available investments. If a particular security tends to have high returns when bad things happen to the investment opportunity set, investors would want to hold this security as a hedge. This increased demand would result in a higher equilibrium price for the security, with all other factors held constant. While the APT gives little guidance as to the number and nature of factors, the factors that appear in the ICAPM satisfy the condition by describing the evolution of the investment opportunity over time and identify the fact that investors are sufficiently concerned about these factors and want to hedge against their effects.

For example, this explains why there might be a price factor for unexpected changes in the real market interest rate. Such a change would clearly cause a shift in the investment opportunity set, and the impact would be pervasive enough that all rational investors would want to protect themselves from the negative consequences. No one yet tells us exactly how many factors there are, but the ICAPM at least gives us some guidance.

The CAPM and its various subtle flavors, as previously described, have since become the departure point for many academic studies that attempt to identify the specific factors that impact the capital asset pricing equation within the markets. These factors are then often studied in relation to their separate impact on large and small stocks. The result of this is a large body of academic work that supports CAPM and its variants and an equally large body of work that raises many questions about the validity of the work. Within these contradictory studies is found some very interesting work about small and micro cap stocks.

Another scholar, Rolf Banz, discovered an apparent contradiction of the CAPM. In his work, Banz shows that the stocks of firms with small market capitalization have higher average returns than large cap stocks. Proponents of the CAPM will point out that small firms tend to have higher betas than large firms, so we would expect to see higher average returns for small firms. However, Banz shows that the beta differences are not large enough to explain the observed return differences. Other academic work shows that the smaller the market cap, the more pronounced the unexplained difference becomes.

From Banz, the body of academic literature begins to develop a framework that suggests that small and micro cap stocks behave differently than their large cap counterparts. A growing body of academic research suggests that certain structural issues related to transaction costs have a large impact on small and micro cap stocks. According to a study done by Andre Perold ("The Implementation Shortfall: Paper versus Reality," *Journal of Portfolio Management*, Spring 1988), there are four elements of transaction costs that affect the efficiency of a stock's return: commissions, taxes, market impact, and opportunity cost. Commissions and taxes are relatively simple to estimate, while market impact and opportunity costs can be difficult to quantify. Market impact is the change in a stock's price due to trading volume that is larger than the stock's typical average trading volume. The idea is that bigger-than-average buying or selling volume in a given stock can disrupt the normal market clearing process, causing changes in the bid-and-ask spread and resulting in performance loss because the investor must buy at a higher price or sell at a lower price due to the abnormal trading volume.

Opportunity cost is the theoretical cost of not completing a trade within a specific time frame. For example, a portfolio manager who wanted to buy 50,000 shares of a given stock that trades 5,000 shares per day could be faced with opportunity cost. The manager could attempt to buy the stock more quickly, creating an increase in the bid-and-ask spread and resulting in higher market impact costs, or the investor could take 10 or more days to complete the trade at the normal average daily trading volume.

But the stock might increase in price during those 10 days because of fundamental or market events. The loss in performance over that period during which the 50,000-share position was being filled is the opportunity cost. Because micro cap stocks trade with less frequency and in smaller volumes than larger stocks, micro cap investors should be aware of both market impact and the opportunity cost of their potential trades.

An interesting study done by Merrill Lynch examined the historical performance of stocks by market capitalization. The study followed a universe of 6,000 stocks on a quarter-by-quarter basis. The performance was broken down by market capitalization and rebalanced annually from 1974 through 1993. A summary of the return and risk measures for each quarter is presented in Table 3-1.

In reviewing the data, it is apparent that risk, as measured by standard deviation, increases as returns increase. These observations are consistent with the CAPM, as discussed earlier in this section. However, a number of studies have shown that when measuring risk using the Sharpe ratio, mid cap stocks provide the best risk-adjusted return. The Sharpe ratio is simply the amount of return achieved for each unit of risk or standard deviation undertaken. But micro cap stocks provide the second-best Sharpe ratio with just slightly more risks per unit of return than mid cap stocks. It should be noted, however, that both absolute return and the amount of risk as measured by standard deviation of return increase dramatically for micro cap stocks, even though the Sharpe ratio for micro cap versus mid cap appears relatively similar. More important, micro cap returns have a low correlation to mid cap and other broad stock market returns. This makes micro

TABLE 3-1   Risk/Return Characteristics by Market Capitalization, 1974–1993

Market Cap	Annual Return	Standard Deviation	Sharpe Ratio
Large Cap	11.0%	15.9%	0.691
Mid Cap	14.3%	17.3%	0.827
Small Cap	15.4%	19.1%	0.806
Micro Cap	19.0%	23.4%	0.812
Source: Merrill Lynch			

cap stocks an excellent diversification tool in the context of a multiasset class portfolio.

ASSET ALLOCATION AND MODERN PORTFOLIO THEORY

Over the past 20 years, an entire industry has been developed from the simple concept that Markowitz put forth that the majority of the total performance of a portfolio results from the mix of investment asset classes contained in the portfolio. This simple concept is the cornerstone of *modern portfolio theory* (MPT). The industry spawned by the advent of MPT is known as *investment management consulting.* This group of consultants stands ready to advise the investing community on the correct allocation of different investment vehicles that should properly be held in a portfolio to achieve the stated investment policy. As is true of most objectives, there is normally a multitude of ways to achieve the stated goal. Through consultation with the client and study of market history, the investment consultant will design a portfolio allocation model that will drive the investment returns of the client toward a stated goal. The consultant will also assist the investor in developing a stated goal or policy that is consistent with the asset allocation model. Institutional investors such as pension plans, endowments, and wealthy individuals have historically hired investment consultants to address long-term investment objectives and policy questions related to asset allocation issues. These institutional investors have a fiduciary obligation to protect the interest of their investors. One way to protect the interest of their investors as well as reduce their own potential liability is to hire a consultant to monitor the investment-related issues. The consultant's job is to advise the client on the correct mix of investments and monitor the underlying performance of those investments to be certain that they remain consistent with the policy objective.

In the past, the complex mathematics embedded in the consultant's practice, along with the myriad of data required to perform the asset allocation analysis, limited the accessibility of investment consulting to larger institutional investors. However, the rapid growth in the power of the personal computer along with the democratization of data via the Internet and the accessibility of modestly priced statistical software have combined to bring asset allocation modeling within the reach of even the smallest individual investor. Web sites offering asset allocation advice and online calculations have proliferated. Modestly priced financial planning and asset allocation software is widely available. Traditional Wall Street brokerage firms as well as discount brokerage firms have asset allocation investment programs available to their clients in some form. Mutual fund complexes and 401(k) providers often offer asset allocation advice to their clients as well. The practical application and administration of the asset allocation process is more difficult than most people realize. There can be many ways to arrive at the same goal, but there are often practical constraints in getting to the stated objective.

ASSET ALLOCATION AND MICRO CAPS

Total portfolio performance is impacted by three variables that can be attributed to any given investment class:

1. Long-term expected and historical rates of return
2. Volatility of the return, typically referred to as the *standard deviation of return*
3. Correlation of returns to other investments

When considering an asset class as a possible investment in a portfolio, a consultant will first study the rate of return to determine whether the historic and expected returns are high enough to compete with other available investments. This return analysis is then tempered with a review of how volatile the return patterns are over time. The higher the volatility of a potential return, often called *risk*, the higher the required rate of return becomes in order to achieve a position in the investment program. Stated simply, the higher the risk of an investment, the higher the expected return should be. If the expected returns are high enough and the correlation of returns to other investments is low enough, then the potential investment might gain an allocation position within the theoretical portfolio.

The classic implementation of asset allocations is the stock and bond mix of a typical balanced portfolio. Both the stock and the bond asset classes have reasonable expected and historical rates of return over the long term. Bond returns are lower than stock returns, but bond returns are less volatile than stock returns, and the correlation between stocks and bonds is relatively low. So during periods when stocks may be underperforming their historical expected rate of return, bonds have a tendency to outperform their long-term historical rate of return. This trade-off between risk and return tends to lower the volatility of the entire portfolio while increasing the total return for each unit of risk undertaken within the given portfolio.

As seen in Table 3-2, the returns for micro cap stocks are nothing short of spectacular. With an annualized return of 19 percent for the 20-year period from 1974 through 1993, micro caps were the return leader in the equity sector. With a standard deviation of return for the same period of 23.4 percent, they were also the most volatile segment of the equity sector. The micro cap sector also looked favorable over the last 10 years. During the period from 1992 through 2002, micro cap stocks had an average annual return of 11.72 percent with a standard deviation for the same period of 12.1 percent. This continues to compare favorably with other equity market segments, as shown in Table 3-2.

The volatility of micro caps looks favorable when compared to the volatility of small, mid, and large cap stocks as well as bonds. When adjusted for the Sharpe ratio, they move into a tie for first place with mid cap stocks, delivering more return for each unit of risk than any other equity asset class over the last 20, 10, and 5 years. So micro caps can provide very competitive long-term historical rates of return on both an absolute and a risk-adjusted basis.

Although micro caps provide a performance advantage over their larger cap counterparts over time, there are clearly peaks and troughs in their performance. It is important to be aware of these micro cap cycles because investing at cyclical peaks can substantially reduce the return profile over short and intermediate time horizons. The cyclical nature of micro caps is best

TABLE 3-2 Comparative Returns and Volatility of Stocks and Bonds

Time Period	Wilshire Micro Cap		Large Cap S&P 500		Emerging Technology Nasdaq Composite		Small Cap Russell 2000		Bonds Lehman Aggregate	
	Annual Return	Standard Deviation	Standard Deviation	Annual Return	Annual Return	Standard Deviation	Standard Deviation	Annual Return	Annual Return	Standard Deviation
1983–2002	12.3	14.6	12.7	16.4	7.1	19.4	11.6	22.7	11.1	10.5
1993–2002	11.7	12.1	9.3	17.0	7.0	20.8	11.5	23.1	9.7	9.6
1998–2002	6.4	21.2	-0.6	21.6	-3.2	33.5	4.3	29.9	8.8	9.3

measured by comparing the performance of micro caps to the performance of large cap stocks such as the S&P 500. When looking back, it appears there have been nine outperformance cycles since 1926. As can be seen in Table 3-3, during the nine cycles micro cap stocks have provided gains slightly twice those of larger stocks. These outperformance cycles have lasted on average about four years, with the shortest cycle lasting about a year and a half and the longest cycle being over nine years in duration.

The downward cycles can be more pronounced and tend to last longer than the outperformance cycles. During downturns, micro caps have declined an average of 6.5 percent per year, while large stocks have gained on average about 5 percent. This average performance gap of 1,150 basis points can be painful because on average it lasts for nearly five years. Although it should be noted that during half of these underperformance cycles, micro caps actually provided positive investment returns, they were just lower returns than those of large cap stocks. This data is also slightly skewed because of the very large and long declines of the great depression and the micro cap bear market of the early 1970s. Nonetheless, the data show that there are very long periods when micro caps behave very differently than their larger stock cousins.

Due to the volatility of the micro cap sector, there are often some short, sharp corrections within both outperformance and underperformance cycles. These short changes in relative performance tend to last about four months and are often correlated with broader market dips. In these instances, stocks in general tend to be in a downturn, and small stocks tend to suffer by a greater magnitude than large stocks.

It is critical to remember that time is an important ally in the investment process. A dollar invested in micro caps in 1926 would have grown to $5,865 by the end of 2002, while the same dollar invested in the S&P 500 would have grown to $1,226. This is a dramatic result and has the effect of showing some very deep bear markets as well as the subsequent rebounds from those deep troughs. But as seen in Table 3-4, the historical probability of micro caps outperforming large caps is quite high as time horizons expand.

As noted, in over 78 percent of the rolling 120-month periods since 1926, micro cap stocks have outperformed their large cap

TABLE 3-3 Micro Cap Stocks Outperformance Cycles, 1926–2002

Time Period	Duration in Years	Microcap Relative Return	Annual Relative Return	All Stocks	Large Stocks	Mid Cap Stocks	Small Cap Stocks	Micro Cap Stocks
						Actual Absolute Returns		
May 1932–March 1937	4.9	393.6	38.4	31.6	29.2	43.3	56.0	82.1
January 1942–May 1946	4.4	285.2	35.7	26.9	23.8	36.9	48.1	72.2
July 1949–January 1951	1.6	19.5	11.9	39.5	37.8	43.5	51.5	56.1
January 1954–February 1955	1.2	14.6	12.4	46.3	44.4	52.6	55.5	64.1
December 1957–March 1959	1.3	25.3	18.4	30.9	28.1	42.3	47.8	55.1
January 1964–January 1969	5.1	158.5	20.5	11.9	8.8	18.3	25.0	34.9
July 1974–July 1983	9.1	219.0	13.6	14.4	11.4	22.3	27.4	30.0
November 1990–February 1994	3.3	38.5	10.3	19.7	16.4	27.3	29.8	32.0
January 1998–December 2002	5.0	155.4	21.2	0.3	−0.6	1.2	4.3	6.4
Average	4.0	145.5	20.3	24.6	22.1	32.0	38.4	48.1

Source: Uniplan, Inc., and Schroder & Co.

TABLE 3-4 Probability of Micro Cap Stocks Outperforming Large Cap Stocks, Rolling Return Periods, 1926–2002

Rolling Period in Years	Probability of Outperformance
20	98%
15	89%
10	78%
5	54%
3	39%
1	21%

cousins. Even dropping down to any given rolling five-year period, the odds are still better than even that the micro cap sector will outperform. If an investor is willing to make a 20-year commitment, there are only four observations out of 224 rolling 20-year periods, where the return on micro cap stocks was lower than that of large caps. This translates into a better than 98 percent probability that over any given 20-year period, micro caps will outperform large cap stocks.

Economic Linkage

The remaining issue from a portfolio construction point of view is correlation. How do micro caps behave relative to other available investment asset classes?

VENTURE CAPITAL AND PRIVATE EQUITY

Private equity or venture capital is an asset class that large investment institutions have formally embraced as part of their portfolios for the past 50 years. Among institutional investors, it's no secret that high-quality private equity deals provide an excellent long-term return on investment as well as significant portfolio diversification characteristics.

The two principal components of venture capital investing are focused on venture strategies and buyout opportunities. The growth of assets available to fund smaller fast-growth private companies has been the principal focus of venture capital investors for the past decade. The surge in the flow of dollars into the private equity or venture capital arena has been stunning over the past decade (see Figure 3.4).

The opportunity to earn high returns from getting in on the ground floor of new ventures, particularly those with the new economy at their core, has attracted much of this capital. Many of these venture capital opportunities will ultimately find their way into the public markets as a source of liquidity for the venture capital community.

Even though the stories of high returns have gained the attention of investors and the public, the information available on private equity deals continues to be elusive. As the name connotes, information about private equity returns and asset values is typically private and, as a result, difficult to obtain and relatively unreliable. Compare this with the public markets, particularly large capitalization stocks, where disclosure is broad and liquidity is good. This public/private information disparity makes it difficult to draw comparisons of public and private assets. However, there are many similarities between private equities and the micro cap market, where the flow of information and liquidity are much more modest and resemble those of private investing rather than large cap investing. The similarities in information flow and liquidity create a linkage between the private equity market and the micro cap market.

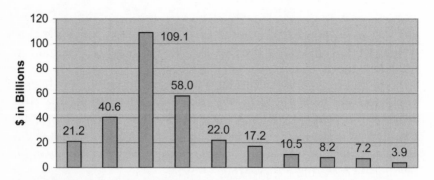

FIGURE 3.4 Venture capital funds raised.

MICRO CAP VERSUS VENTURE CAPITAL

In many ways, the story of venture capital is the story of commerce itself. Every venture capitalist will tell you that the business begins in the fifteenth century, when Christopher Columbus sought to travel westward instead of eastward from Europe to reach India. His visionary idea did not find favor with the king of Portugal, who refused to finance his venture. After visiting many merchant banks, Queen Isabella of Spain decided to "fund" him for his venture. And so the story goes: The concept of venture capital was born.

The modern venture capital industry as we know it today began taking shape in the post–World War II era. In 1946, American Research and Development Corporation was founded with the explicit goal of making investments in promising new companies. They evolved the basic business model for the venture capital industry. Their venture capital investment in Digital Equipment provided them with an astounding 101 percent annualized return on investment. Suddenly, many large capital pools embraced the idea of allocating a portion of their investment capital into new business ventures.

In the mid-1950s, the U.S. government recognized the need for risk capital and promoted small business investment companies (SBICs). This gave rise to an entire era of public SBICs that invested shareholder capital into small private ventures. In the late 1960s, the SBIC industry followed the seven-year slump of the U.S. stock market, and most of the small business investments they made also failed. The situation began to look up in the late 1970s, based on a massive reduction in the capital gains tax rate and a number of high-profile IPOs by venture-backed companies such as Federal Express and Apple Computer.

The public market valuations for small and micro cap firms send a signal to the private equity investor about whether the markets are ready and able to absorb new IPO opportunities. The IPO is potentially the most lucrative exit strategy for the venture capitalist. If the expectation in the small and micro cap arena is of multiple expansions, venture capitalists have a direct market signal to be more aggressive in raising and cultivating opportunities that will ultimately appear in the public markets. This creates a certain boom-and-bust cycle that is an accurate barometer of the outlook for both venture capital and micro cap investments.

Venture capital investing is a long-term proposal. The typical holding period for a private venture capital investment is 3 to 7 years, although many venture capital investment partnerships are structured to last 10 years or longer. So the typical venture capital investor has a long-term time horizon and the ability to be involved in an investment vehicle that may show little opportunity for liquidity over 7 years or more. And because institutional investors are generally the only ones who have the size and scale to make these types of investments, the minimum investment amounts are often $1 million or more. It takes real money just to get to the table in venture capital investing. That is not the case for micro cap investing.

As we have discussed, diversification is important in the context of the overall investment portfolio. It is also important in the context of the venture capital investment. As a venture capital manager described it, most venture capital investment pools are composed of one or two home runs and one or two losers, and the balance are the walking dead! The statistics about venture capital from a number of comprehensive studies confirm that description. About 7 percent of the venture deals in any given pool provide over 50 percent of the portfolio total returns. These would be the home runs. On average, about 15 percent of the deals go broke or produce a total loss of the invested capital. These are the losers. The walking dead are the real problem for the venture capitalist. These are the approximately 40 percent of the deals that produce a loss on the investment or the remaining 38 percent that produce a below hurdle rate of return and that may offer little or no hope for a meaningful exit strategy for the venture capital investor. The ways the probabilities work suggest that single venture capital investment has about a fifty-fifty chance of producing some loss for the investor. The typical fiduciary representing an institutional investor in the venture capital sector normally responds to these odds by being invested across a sufficient number of venture capital pools to create a well-diversified portfolio of venture capital opportunities. In addition, the institutional investor often invests in venture capital pools that target different venture strategies. More on this subject will appear in Chapter 12. These issues are more easily resolved in the context of a single micro cap portfolio. Chapter 4 will discuss strategies for adding the micro cap sector to your investment portfolio.

The Micro Cap Asset Class and Portfolio Construction

This chapter will attempt to answer the following questions:

- Can micro cap stocks add value to a multiasset class portfolio?
- What is the correct allocation to micro cap stocks in a typical portfolio?

Let's briefly summarize why micro caps might be of interest to a small institutional or individual investor looking for higher returns and added portfolio diversification. In looking at the opportunities among U.S. domestic stocks, there is a group of stocks that numbers roughly twice as many as small cap stocks. They are micro cap stocks. Some of these companies will expand in market capitalization to the size where they will become of interest to the thousands of small cap managers who manage billions of dollars in portfolio assets. The opportunity to own these companies in advance of that growth would likely provide significant returns for an investor.

However, the efficient market theory suggests that it is not possible for an investor to outperform an index of stocks over a long period of time. But as the market capitalization of stocks becomes smaller, the EMT becomes more questionable. In fact, it appears that a diligent investor can gain an information advantage when dealing with very small public companies. This information advantage seems to be explained when examined in the context of the venture capital theory known as the *principal agent problem.*

It is also well known that over time smaller stocks provide higher returns than larger stocks. This is consistent with the capital asset pricing model and the idea that investors require higher returns for taking larger risks. Risk as measured by volatility of return grows larger as stocks get smaller. However, modern portfolio theory (MPT) suggests that by mixing certain highly volatile asset classes together the risk within a portfolio can be reduced. This has to do with how these risky asset classes behave or correlate relative to one another. The good news is that micro cap stocks appear to be sensitive to broad economic cycles and don't seem to have a very high correlation to either larger stocks or bonds. Thus the micro cap asset class can be an excellent diversification tool within a multiasset class portfolio.

Micro cap stocks not only provide added diversification, but also provide very competitive returns on an absolute and risk-adjusted basis. They outperform larger stocks 78 percent of the time when looked at over a 10-year period and 98 percent of the time when taken over a 20-year period. When compared to venture capital, micro cap stocks appear to have a similar return profile. This is likely due to the relationship between the venture capital sector and the market for initial public offerings of company stock.

The cumulative effect of these stocks leads to the conclusion that micro cap stocks are in many ways a bridge between the public and private capital markets. They behave more like private equity capital in terms of their pricing mechanisms and their correlation to other asset classes. This creates the opportunity for small investors to add an asset class to their portfolios that behaves like private venture capital but has the advantage of some amount of daily liquidity and market-based pricing.

MICRO CAPS IN THE PORTFOLIO ASSET ALLOCATION

The notion of asset allocation has increased in complexity and scope over the past decade. In the beginning it was stocks versus bonds and how much of each was appropriate for a given investor. Over time, many other asset classes were introduced. Oftentimes these other asset classes were recognized because they started out in the portfolios of a narrow group of institutional investors. As the diversification benefit of these asset classes became more widely known, they moved into a larger number of investors' portfolios. Over time, indexes were created to track the performance of these new asset classes, and the investments became available to an ever larger number of smaller investors.

Real estate is a good example of this asset class evolution. When originally introduced to institutional investors, only the largest and most progressive used real estate in their portfolios. As real estate's low correlation to stocks and bonds became better known, the asset class found its way into a larger number of institutional portfolios. Over time, no self-respecting fiduciary would have a diversified portfolio if it did not include real estate. The emergence of the real estate investment trust (REIT) asset class over the past 20 years has made it possible for smaller investors to enjoy the benefits of owning an interest in a diversified portfolio of real estate. Now even the smallest retail investors can include a REIT mutual fund among their holdings and have the positive diversification of real estate. In many ways, the emergence of the micro cap asset class will allow smaller investors to benefit from the diversification of venture capital through the inclusion of micro cap investments in their portfolios just as the emergence of REITs as an asset class has allowed a similar diversification into real estate. The largest and most sophisticated institutional investors have allocated a portion of their portfolios to venture capital. A study done by Uniplan Consulting found that as of December 31, 2003, pension plans in the $1 billion to $10 billion range had allocated on average 7 percent of their assets to venture capital. This was down from 11 percent as of December 31, 1999, which was likely the peak of venture capital investing among these institutions, and that peak largely coincided with the peak in technology and Internet investing.

The Portfolio Contribution of Micro Caps

The simplest way to demonstrate the contribution of micro caps to the asset allocation process is to look at some simple what-if simulations involving micro cap stocks along with other large asset classes. In this instance, the portfolio benefit of micro caps is examined, but the analysis can easily extend to showing the benefit of other asset classes such as international stocks and real estate investment trusts. The examples are designed to be simple and to prove the case that micro caps as an asset class add value in the multiasset portfolio.

In the case of real-life asset allocation situations, consultants and fiduciaries put constraints on the minimum and maximum asset allocation for any given asset class. The specific investment policy and existing nature of the portfolio dictate these constraints. The tax status of a portfolio may have an effect on the amount of income-producing assets that might be targeted for a portfolio. In a taxable portfolio, the allocation may be skewed more heavily toward investments that produce capital gains such as common stocks. In a tax-exempt portfolio, it is likely that the policy guidelines might be more biased toward higher allocations of income-producing assets. Total asset size is also a potential factor when considering allocation targets. Very large institutional portfolios may not be able to effectively use smaller and less liquid asset classes such as micro caps as a part of their overall strategy due to their varying size or liquidity needs.

With the goal of avoiding overly complex math, it is worth examining the potential portfolio contribution of micro caps by constructing a simple set of what-if portfolios using stocks, bonds, and micro caps. These what-if portfolio simulations take simple allocations and add micro caps in varying amounts over differing time periods in an attempt to determine their potential investment contribution to portfolio performance. In this simulation we use the following asset classes. Large stocks are represented by the S&P 500, and bonds are represented by the Lehman Intermediate Government Corporate Bond Index, both of which are very large liquid benchmarks used by institutional investors. Micro cap stocks are represented by the Wilshire Micro Cap Index, an unmanaged index of micro cap stocks that represents the smallest 10 percent of market capitalization in the Wilshire 5000, a broad-based U.S. stock market index. The time period used is the 25 years ended December 31, 2003, which is about as far back as the Wilshire Micro Cap Index extends.

The what-if scenario begins using the classic balanced portfolio that is 60 percent stocks and 40 percent bonds. This case would have provided the investor a return of 7.7 percent, with an annual standard deviation of 13.3 percent before fees and expenses. This is the de facto generic standard balanced portfolio that is used almost universally as the point of departure for institutional portfolio performance measurement. The question is then posed: How would the outcome have differed if the portfolio contained micro cap stocks? For our purposes, we will add micro cap stocks in 5 percent increments to the portfolio while lowering the stock component by a similar amount. The outcome is shown in Table 4-1.

It is remarkable to see that by simply adding the first 5 percent allocation of micro caps, the overall return in the portfolio jumps to 8.2 percent while the annual volatility drops modestly to 12.7 percent. Thus, a very modest allocation of micro caps begins to have an immediate and substantial positive impact on the standard balanced portfolio. Moving the allocation of micro caps to 10 percent continues to add benefit as the annual return moves up to 8.7 percent, but more important, the annual standard deviation drops sharply to 11.6 percent, a 100-basis-point decrease in

TABLE 4-1 Microcap Contribution, Stock Bond Portfolio, 25 years as of 12/31/03

Allocation				
Stocks	**Bonds**	**Microcaps**	**Annual Return**	**Standard Deviation**
60	40	0	7.7%	13.3%
55	40	5	8.2%	12.7%
50	40	10	8.7%	11.6%
45	40	15	9.2%	10.6%
40	40	20	9.6%	9.9%
35	40	25	10.2%	9.3%
30	40	30	10.6%	9.0%
25	40	35	10.9%	8.8%
20	40	40	11.1%	8.6%
15	40	45	11.2%	8.9%

Stocks S&P 500; Bonds Lehman Government Corporation; Microcaps Wilshire Microcap.

overall portfolio volatility. As shown Table 4.1, the return continues to increase and volatility begins to drop as each incremental unit of micro cap is added. The volatility of the portfolio continues to decline until micro caps reach 42 percent of the allocation, at which point the volatility begins to rise. Thus, from a purely theoretical point of view, returns increase and volatility declines up to a 42 percent allocation. From a practical point of view, it is unlikely that any institutional investor with responsibilities as a fiduciary would recommend that a client carry an allocation of 42 percent micro cap stocks. However, it is relatively simple to demonstrate in most allocation studies that a 5 percent to 20 percent allocation in micro caps can increase overall portfolio return while lowering volatility.

CONCLUSION

In the world of equity-based returns it is easy to conclude, based on the data presented, that micro cap stocks offer an attractive risk/reward trade-off. With a volatility profile slightly higher than that of both large cap and small cap stocks, but with significantly higher return opportunities, it is logical to consider micro caps as a part of the overall portfolio allocation strategy. A low correlation of returns to bonds and other asset classes helps reduce risk and increase overall returns in most portfolios. With many of the fundamental characteristics of venture capital and a return profile that looks more like venture capital than plain common stocks, it is reasonable for the small investor to consider micro caps as a logical substitute for the venture capital asset class.

CHAPTER 5

Using the Information Advantage

This chapter will attempt to answer the following questions:

- Can principal agent theory help to identify micro cap opportunities?
- What company-specific items should an investor consider?

METHODS TO EVALUATE PRINCIPAL AGENT ACTIONS

If the principal agent theory holds true, there are two groups of investors whose actions should be watched closely when you are looking for micro cap opportunities. Company insiders who are the principals of the transaction are the first group to watch. Knowledgeable institutional investors who are the agents in venture capital theory are the other group to watch. Observing the actions of these groups is very difficult to do within the venture capital community. Venture capital, being private in nature, allows only limited transparency with regard to investment activities. However, the public capital markets are much more transparent, and therein exists the opportunity to gain an information advantage.

Management, Management, Management

As in any business, the quality of the management is a key factor in determining the success of the enterprise. In most cases, the skill and vision of the key management team will determine the long-term success of an enterprise. And the smaller a company, the larger the impact of the top management team. In a micro cap company, the top tier of key management people has a disproportionately large influence on the success or failure of the company. Unlike large companies, in most micro cap organizations the key management people also have direct responsibility for actual business execution. This is an important difference between the big and the small enterprise. Success in the micro cap world requires a certain management skill set that merges big corporate vision with a high level of entrepreneurship. So in micro cap companies, for practical purposes, the single largest contributing factor in corporate performance is attributable to the top management team. This suggests that finding opportunities in the micro cap world requires a complete and careful evaluation and analysis of key management.

Because the micro cap universe is so large, there is some level of basic screening that is required to arrive at a working universe of companies to consider for investment purposes. In the micro cap world, there are very few sell-side research analysts to provide ongoing research support and evaluation of micro cap companies. In addition, those analysts who do cover these companies are often more junior members of the research team and not as experienced or as insightful as their more senior counterparts who cover larger companies. In addition, the analysts who cover micro cap companies often focus their attention on the professional portfolio managers that specialize in micro cap stocks. This makes it more difficult for the average investor to get high-quality research on micro cap companies.

However, there is one key group of people who are very close to the company whose actions can provide a leading indicator of investment opportunity in the micro cap sector. They are the material insiders of the company who make up the top management team along with the officers and directors of the company. This key group should be studied very closely when looking for micro cap opportunities. An evaluation of the corporate management team is often the key to detecting and discovering potential changes at a company before they are generally fully reflected in the valuation of the underlying stock. There are some very effective methods to monitor the ongoing actions of the management of a large group of micro cap companies for patterns that could indicate positive future events for the company.

The buying and selling patterns of the key management team can be a stunning leading indicator of a company's future prospects. Who else is in a better position to make a critical evaluation about the future business prospects of a company? The key management team will have firsthand knowledge of the day-to-day operations of the company and how they are progressing. In addition, the insiders have a keen awareness of the current valuation of the company. Who better to make an informed principal agent decision about the current value and future prospects of the company than the existing key management personnel? The pattern of their buying and selling can be a very powerful indicator of future stock performance. Also, these material insiders are required to disclose their purchase and sale decisions to the public at large in a timely manner through filings with the SEC. The review of these filings can be a powerful tool for screening the micro cap universe for investment opportunities.

WHO'S DOING WHAT: INSIDER INFORMATION

Public companies are required to file a number of documents each year with the Securities and Exchange Commission in Washington, D.C. These filings are required by statute to promote full and fair disclosure about company-level information. A set of these same filing requirements extends beyond the company to certain shareholders of the company. The largest groups of these shareholders are the management insiders of the company. The SEC defines an insider as an officer or director of a public company. In addition, an insider can be a legal entity or individual who directly or indirectly owns 10 percent or more of any class of a company's shares. These are presumed by the SEC to be people who possess a much higher level of knowledge about a company and its current and future prospects. Once an individual or entity meets the criteria to be considered an insider, the SEC becomes interested in monitoring how you traffic in the buying and selling of your company shares. To monitor the activity of insiders, the SEC has certain specific reporting requirements that apply to insiders. These requirements come in the form of certain disclosures about stock ownership that must be made on Forms 3, 4, and 5 as detailed in the federal regulations concerning the SEC.

The rules require that an insider must make an initial filing of his or her holdings of the company stock within 10 days of becoming an insider. Form 3, disclosing those holdings, must be filed with the SEC within that 10-day period. The form must be filed even if the insider owns no shares.

After the insider files Form 3, any changes in his or her stock holdings of the company must be filed with the SEC on Form 4. The SEC must receive this form not later than the tenth of the month following the insider activity. For example, any insider trades made during March must be filed on Form 4 and received by the SEC no later than April 10.

All insiders must file Form 5 within 45 days of the company's fiscal year-end. Form 5 details certain transactions that are not required to be reported on Form 4, such as dividend reinvestments. Any person or entity who was an insider during the fiscal year, but is no longer an insider, must also file Form 5 for the prior year. So any insiders who left during the fiscal year must report their subsequent share activity through the fiscal year-end on Form 5.

Although Forms 3 and 5 can be helpful when studying the activities of a company and its insiders, the Form 4 data is usually the most useful and important to outside investors. It can frequently be a treasure trove of information for analyzing the future prospects of a company. Form 4 discloses to investors on a continuous basis how insiders regard their company and its future prospects. As this book discusses later, having a management team with meaningful share ownership is a good indicator that the interests of shareholders and management will be better aligned. But knowing when insiders are buying and selling meaningful amounts of shares in the open market is normally a strong indicator of current share value and a barometer of management's opinion of future company prospects.

When examining insider trading data, it is important to focus on open-market trades. These are the buys and sells of management that are done in the open market at the then current market prices. They are the most important trades because they reflect the actual outlook of the insider with respect to the market value and future prospects of the company. Insiders who are actively buying or selling shares without linkage to options are sending a strong indication of their insider knowledge to the market. If the transactions are not related to the exercise of options connected to the company's option benefit plan, then the insider believes that the price of the stock is high or low, or that the future prospects are improving or declining.

This is much more important when considering buys versus sells. There are often a possible myriad of reasons why people sell stock over and above the belief that the shares are overpriced. Buying houses, paying taxes, funding tuition for children, and so forth, are all valid reasons to liquidate holdings in an asset. The one exception to the general notion that selling is not as important is that of selling after a large stock price decline. And this is more important when groups of managers are selling in clusters after a large share-price decline. It is logical to assume that most rational investors would not sell shares after a large share-price decline unless they felt that the shares were going to decline further in price. Thus, management clusters selling after a significant share-price decline is a very negative indicator of share valuation and future outlook for a micro cap stock. Conversely, insider buying is often a good indication that share valuations are low in the opinion of management or that business and industry performance is improving. Why else would management shell out real cash to buy shares in the open market? It is a place for the share price to move higher. And in the case of insider buying, size is important. Size is relative, but it is much more significant to see a corporate insider buy $100,000 of stock versus $10,000. Both purchases are significant, but the message is much stronger in the larger transaction.

Although size is important, there are some qualifiers to consider. It is worth taking a look at the track record of the insider's previous open-market share purchases. Does the insider display a strong track record of making open-market purchases that translate into gains? Or is the insider less insightful in the timing of purchases? When making this analysis, it is important to review the data over a longer time horizon. All the data show that the insiders who buy, and particularly those who do it well, are often early with their share purchases. It is best to look at a period of at least nine months to a year when analyzing insider purchases. Also, as in insider selling, it is often worthwhile to look for groups or clusters of management activity. It is significant when the chief executive officer buys $100,000 of stock, but it is more important when management and directors as a team buy $1 million of stock, particularly when this happens during a concentrated time period. This is often an indicator of very substantial events about to take place.

A complete evaluation of the management could require a number of meetings at several different times. However, it is possible to select the most relevant ideas for whatever company you are researching and in a short period of time form a reliable first impression of the quality of management. The payoff from this fundamental research is the ability to come to a conclusion about the quality of management. An uncommon company is likely to be run by uncommon people. It is important to conclude from your analysis that you have a strong confidence level in the management of a micro cap company prior to owning its stock.

However, the evaluation of management should be twofold. First, it enables the investor to form an opinion about the quality of the company's management. Second, it allows investors to build important lines of communication with the top management team of the micro cap company. In communicating with management, there are a number of facts that you will want to discover as you get to know the management and assess the company. Number one, who are the top managers? The key management people who actually make the decisions about the long-term strategy of the company are the top management people. It is typical for the highest titles to be given to the same people who carry out those top functions. However, there are times when titles are misplaced. At some companies, the reality may be that the CEO is the treasurer of the company, or the true leader of the company may be the chief production officer. The title of president and chief executive officer may reside with somebody else; however, that person may not in fact be the true top decision maker within the company. Although that chief executive may have the final word on major decisions, the other executives may in fact be the brain trust of the company.

Most companies, both big and small, proudly publish the resumes of their key operating people. It is worthwhile to obtain these from the company if they are available and save them in a company file. It's useful to look for a broad pattern of facts in the resumes of the executive management teams. The resume can also help you judge the scope and pattern of outside connections a given key manager may have. In some instances, a clear pattern can be seen among the members of the key management team. They may have worked together previously at other companies, or they may have the same educational background, having attended the same university. In addition, it may be possible to spot subtle nuances of a management team's historical outcomes. For example, it is not unusual to see a chief executive officer who has engineered the sale of the last few companies where he or she was also the CEO. This can be an indication that the CEO has a "fix it up, dress it up" outlook that often leads to the near-term sale of the company, hopefully at a higher price. After a while, these executives become worth tracking if they have done a good job in the subsequent sale of other companies. As discussed, in many cases the ultimate outcome at the corporate level is in large part related directly to the key management team. If the management team has a history of selling companies, this may be of interest to you as an investor. In fact, people who have come from an investment banking background often transform themselves into the role of chief executive with the express goal of dressing up and fixing up a company for sale. It is worthwhile to take special note of key management people who have a background or history in the investment banking area.

It is also worthwhile to know and understand how a company's key activities are organized. To best understand the business, it is worth taking some time to study the organizational chart of the company. The way the organizational chart appears on paper may not actually reflect the way things function at the company. It's worth attempting to make this determination when discussing the company with management. It is also helpful to study an organizational chart of the affiliated companies that might be owned by the micro cap. These affiliated and subsidiary companies can often lead to discoveries about hidden technologies and hidden value within the micro cap company. Studying the organizational chart can also help you to understand how pivotal business decisions flow through the organization.

For example, a retail company that is in a growth and expansion mode may be required to select dozens of potential retail sites each year to continue an expansion. These decisions are key to the future success of the retail organization's growth. In that scenario, it would be important to know and understand who ultimately makes the real estate location decisions for that retail micro cap company. In some instances, such as finding retail locations, it may be better to have a single person with the appropriate skill set focused on that activity rather than attempting to select sites by committee. It is important to determine that the key person in question has been successful in the past at executing the job and continues to execute successfully in the future. There are other situations, however, that may benefit from a broader, more structured team approach to decision making. It is important to look for companies where the members of the key management team seem to have the ability to communicate among one another effectively rather than having a single executive surrounded by a group of executives who are afraid to disagree or discuss openly the issues surrounding a particular decision or strategy.

It is useful to understand that at times key decisions may have little or no impact on the long-term outlook for the company. In some circumstances, companies may have little control over their own destiny, and even the most thoughtful decisions will have little or no major effect on the ongoing profitability of the concern. For example, in commodity-oriented companies, where many price decisions are driven by supply and demand in the marketplace, few operating decisions may have a large relative impact on the company. In many instances, these companies are highly leveraged to market pricing, and their operating earnings are highly leveraged to those market prices.

Frequently, these very companies are not of much interest to the broader investing community. However, it is often possible to forecast with a relatively high degree of competence the direction of some of the external market factors that impact these companies. We will discuss in greater detail these highly leveraged operating companies and simple ways to try to capitalize on operating cycles within specific industries.

MANAGEMENT STYLE

It is often important to try to make an assessment of management style. Does management have certain prejudices or theories regarding the appropriate method of conducting the particular business? Is the management approach very centralized, with a distinctive top-down style, much like a military organization? Or does it appear that the management style is more collaborative with regard to the decision-making process? Is there an open flow of information in both directions, or does information seem to emanate mostly from the top down or from the bottom up? It's difficult to assert that either management style is more or less appropriate. Because it is a highly subjective area, it is often anecdotal indications that lead to a conclusion about the effectiveness of management. Do employees seem engaged and interested? How do employees treat potential clients and how does that compare to the manner in which they treat existing clients? Talking to rank-and-file workers within the company can lead to very interesting comments, both positive and negative. It is important to weigh these anecdotal factors when evaluating the management culture.

STRATEGY AND PLANNING SYSTEMS

Long-term planning and strategy are the key to management's ability to grow and maintain a business. A strategy and planning system creates a framework within which information is gathered and processed inside the business. It sets a fundamental basis for how future plans and expectations are formulated and related to one another. In addition, the way the corporate structure is built to gather operating data and relay those data back to management, where the management team can compare the information to their framework of expectations, is particularly important. Flat organizational structures that have very quick feedback loops tend to be able to adjust operating strategies much more quickly than larger, more hierarchical organizations.

It is useful to discuss with management its internal reporting requirements and procedures. Find out how often data are gathered and transmitted to key management personnel. In addition, attempt to determine how those data are evaluated relative to the strategic and operating plans and try to determine what actions are prescribed to be taken and by whom when the data are not consistent with the operating plan. A good organization will have many planning and control systems in place to evaluate many levels of corporate data. However, it's not just the quantity of data gathered but rather the quality of data that is important in a successful feedback loop. In addition, good timely data that are not used effectively are also of no benefit to management. It is worth spending some time to learn the ways that these systems were developed. In addition, it's worthwhile to ask management about the internal checks and balances that are used to ensure the quality of the data and that the information is being used and evaluated correctly. Does it seem that management has too many or too few reports? Does management have one comprehensive enterprise-level information system, or are there a number of systems operating independently that require integration of data in order to get sufficient reports for management? These are all key questions that should be discussed and analyzed with management.

It is important to discuss with management how compensation is related to the planning system. What are the consequences of deviating from the plan? What actions are taken as a result of variances within the plan, and how much latitude does management have with regard to these variances? How far off budget can a manager get before running into trouble? Is compensation related to simply making sales numbers, or are margins and profitability factors when evaluating compensation? These are all important issues that have no simple answers; however, they need to be reviewed in the context of the business plan to determine whether in fact there are effective controls.

MANAGEMENT CHANGES

Changes in key management personnel are often a leading indicator of a change in company performance. It is worth investigating very carefully the reasons and rationale behind any recent changes in the top management team. In addition, it can be very beneficial to speak with any top managers who have recently left the company. It is important to try to understand the context of these management changes.

It can be very tempting to buy shares in a company that has recently had a major change in management. However, it's important to remember that if a company has problems of the magnitude that required a change of management, it is likely they will not be solved quickly. The replacement of a handful of key operating people is often an early indicator that major changes at the company may be about to take place. In many cases, this new management team must not only assess the company itself but also change the fundamental management culture within the company. In most instances, the real tangible impact of a management change is not reflected in the operating performance of the company until several years have gone by. It is very common for the new, incoming management team to make substantial financial adjustments including writing off every single questionable item on the books in order to clear the decks for the financial reporting going forward. In addition, it is likely that there will be substantial turnover within the middle management ranks of the company as the new management team evaluates the quality of the existing management structure and begins to make changes to that structure. Finally, the new management team must then convince the existing workforce to embrace the new operating strategy and work under a new management culture going forward. It can easily take two or three years for these changes to be reflected in the operating performance of the company. However, these early changes are a good indicator and generally suggest closer scrutiny of the operating performance of the company going forward. That additional scrutiny can often lead to excellent opportunities as new management begins to improve the operating performance of the company.

MANAGEMENT REPUTATION

Does management have a clear strategy or plan? And how is this plan received by members of the investment community? Of course, it is not uncommon for any management team to want to give you a positive story about their future expectations for growth and profitability. Whatever the current plan, it is important to evaluate how management has executed similar plans in the past. Do they have a history of disappointing their shareholders and analysts? Have they overpromised and underdelivered in the past? Or have they met the expectations as promoted in their forecasts and outlook? This goes to the very important issue of management credibility.

A management team that has consistently disappointed shareholders and investors and has come up short repeatedly on a historical basis will often see the price of their shares at a discount to their industry peers as a result of their poor performance. Conversely, management teams that have been honest in their future assessment of operating conditions and relatively consistent in meeting the expectations as laid out in their forecasts will often carry a premium to the valuation of a group. Once the reputation of a management team has been established, it is hard to change the opinion on Wall Street, whether that be negative or positive.

HOW THE COMPANY DEVELOPS AND PROMOTES EMPLOYEES

As a long-term shareholder, it is important to know and understand what provisions are being made to attract good people who can replace key managers as this becomes necessary over time. The manner in which companies develop and promote people can give an important indication of the quality of the management culture. In today's world of high-performance corporations, key spots will have to be filled from either existing middle management staff or through outside connections the company already has with industry professionals. Developing a talent pool within the management ranks is an important factor for most small companies. At issue here is whether managers have access and exposure to the top people within the corporation and whether the top people within the corporation are willing to devote time and energy to training and understanding their middle management ranks.

Some candid conversations with midlevel employees can give a good indication of how the company stacks up in this regard. Why do people work there? What do they like about the job? What do they dislike? What would cause them to move on? And, importantly, how do they actually spend their time while at work? These simple questions can give a true sense of how the rank-and-file employees feel about upper management.

CONCLUSION

Your intuitive feelings about the research process can hold the key to uncovering quality management teams. Reflect on the feelings that arise in reaction to your various conversations with management. Did the key people convey a sense of energy and excitement, and did they answer your questions directly or were they evasive? Did they volunteer information or was it difficult to obtain even the most basic facts? Would you want to hire or work with the key management team? In many ways, when you buy stock in the company, you are buying a share in the management team, and you should feel comfortable owning that share of the management. The intuitive reaction occurs normally in people. Rather than suppressing these intuitive reactions, allow them to move into the front of your thought process and consider them a useful resource.

CHAPTER 6

Corporate Governance

This chapter will attempt to answer the following questions:

- How can a micro cap investor find and use principal agent information?
- What information resources are available to micro cap investors?

In evaluating a company, an enormous amount of information can be gathered simply by examining the parties with whom the company is associated. The outside institutions a company selects can be very helpful in determining the general quality of the company. In general, there should be a meaningful fit between the outside resources and the company itself. These outside resources are nonmanagement members of the board of directors. Directorships held by existing management in other companies, foundations, government boards, or nonprofit organizations; the company's commercial banker; the company's investment banking affiliations; the company's independent outside auditors; and the law firms that represent the company can all give important indications about the company and its spheres of influence. These key constituencies can also tell an awful lot about management's general attitude and inclination toward shareholders.

In today's highly charged atmosphere of business governance, the independent outside members of the board of directors should be scrutinized. Does the board appear to be a collection of friends of the CEO, or do they appear to be a group of independent people who could be an asset to the company in providing certain expertise and guidance in the overall management of the business? Remember, the independent outside trustees are charged with the fiduciary responsibility of supervising management in the context of the best interests of the shareholders. The board of directors should be evaluated carefully to determine whether each member is truly independent and looking out for the best interests of the shareholders.

It can also be very telling to examine the directorships held by members of the existing management team and inside managers at the company. Because of the fiduciary obligation of any director, there is the potential of personal liability being associated as an independent outside director. So the fact that an executive would accept a directorship in another company should reflect a great deal about that individual. It is not unusual to find indications of very strong competence in connection with management people who may serve on outside boards. There are instances when outside directorships will lead inside management to other highly placed executives who can be a resource to that management as well as an invaluable contact. However, you may also find that key executives are busy raising money for charitable organizations or spending large amounts of time on the local school board, and those commitments need to be weighed against their focus on managing the activities of the company. A sure indication of this type of distraction is the executive who may list a large number of public and private board directorships. Conversely, another caution flag can be the management team that appears to have little or no outside engagements with other boards, either public or private. This can be the sign of an inwardly focused management team that lacks a grasp of the key issues of corporate governance. This is not to say that any of this is either good or bad—just that it is another factor that should be evaluated when reviewing a company as a potential investment.

The company's banking relationships should also show the correct fit with the company. Federal filings and annual reports do not always disclose which banks a company has financial relationships with. Normally, most companies are forthcoming in telling you which banking institutions they deal with. A company should deal with a bank that is large enough to handle the financial needs of the corporation, but the relationship with the bank also should be of the correct size and scale to be meaningful and not one where the company is a very small client of a very large bank. In today's current financial environment, banking relationships are far more fluid and flexible than they have been historically. Nevertheless, a strong banking relationship is a critical aspect for most micro cap companies and should be considered in that regard.

The company's investment banker should follow a similar paradigm to that of the company's commercial banker. A quality investment banking relationship can help the company to access capital markets in a timely and efficient way. In addition, the investment banking relationship may provide the opportunity for the company to obtain sell-side research coverage that can be critical in helping to maximize shareholder value in small and micro cap companies. Beyond that, the investment banker can act as an intermediary in the case of a potential acquisition or a potential merger with another company that may help enhance shareholder value. Again, it is the fit of the relationship that should be examined with most care. When discussing strategy with a management team, it is fair to ask the nature of their investment banking relationships. Are there investment bankers on retainer or who are paid a regular fee? It's also fair to ask what their investment bankers have done for them in the past few years. The answer to that question should give you a pretty clear indication of the strength of the company's investment banking relationship.

THE COMPANY'S SOCIAL RELATIONSHIPS

Like people, companies form and maintain certain social relationships. In some companies there is a single family that dominates the management ranks. If this is the case, it normally creates a pattern of corporate governance that revolves around family ties. This may not be bad; however, it can stifle new ideas and discourage bright and aggressive but unconnected people from joining the firm. In a powerful, well-connected family, nepotism among the ranks in the firm can be a great asset. However, as we will see, in some instances it can literally be a disaster for the company.

Another typical pattern is that of school-based relationships. In many instances, graduates of large, top-tier private business schools such as Harvard, Stanford, Yale, and MIT will typically have a bias toward recruiting and hiring key management people who have also attended these schools. If a firm seems to be dominated by graduates of a single school, it can be a red flag for evaluating the management culture. Sometimes it indicates that the management team is not interested in ideas or concepts that go beyond the bounds of what they believe was taught in their affiliated business school.

The same social and school patterns can also be detected with regard to other major cultural beliefs within management. Certain management teams may seem to be focused on religion, ethnic background, political affiliations, or gender. It's not uncommon to see top management teams within companies that are dominated by a particular ethnic background, for example, Italian-American or African-American teams. It is also not unusual to see management teams that are dominated by a single religious affiliation, such as a predominately Jewish management team. Some companies have strong ties to either the Republican or the Democratic Party, and some management teams have a high percentage of male or female members. These biases can be the result of the environment in which the business itself operates and should be considered in that context. So it is worth asking this question: Do the similar backgrounds work better together and relate more easily to those within the company and within the industry?

INFORMATION RESOURCES

The following is a checklist of potential information resources to use when researching a micro cap investment.

- The company
- Federal regulatory filings made by the company

- Competitors of the company
- Customers of the company
- Suppliers to the company
- Industry trade associations
- Sell-side research analysts
- Buy-side research analysts
- Newspapers, magazines, and other publications
- Internet searches
- Briefs and related legal documents filed in public lawsuits

The Company

For practical purposes, anyone within the company at any level can give you a starting point for a research discussion. It is ideal to eventually meet the key senior management officers within the company. The investor relations officer can frequently be the most helpful individual with regard to gaining access to key management personnel.

Former employees are always a wealth of information about a company. They might also be upset and angry with management, and this should be considered when you are listening to what former employees have to say about a company. Most often, former employees are overlooked, yet they are more likely to talk openly about a company than current employees. It is normally possible to find a company's former employees through an industry or trade association Internet web site. In addition, the previous year's annual reports and federal filings will show changes in officers and directors. It is fair to ask the company about these people and how you can contact them. When dealing with former employees, it is important to be honest with them and tell them that you are considering making an investment in the company, that you have no connection with the company or the management of the company, and that everything that you discuss will be off the record and private.

In addition, through networking within the industry, you may be able to find someone who was offered a senior-level job at the company but turned down the offer. This contact can be invaluable because the person can often lend an insider's view of the company's position and strategy within the industry, even though the contact is, in fact, an outsider. The job rejecter's reasons for not joining the firm may not be relevant; however, as an industry participant his or her insights into the firm can be very useful.

Competitors

Normally, the easiest place to find a company's competitors is within industry directories and on industry web sites. Competitors can often provide the most valuable insights into a company. Interestingly enough, sales and marketing people tend to be the most useful resources among competitors. They typically know the marketplace very well and understand the dynamics of what's driving business within the markets they deal with. In addition, the generally open and gregarious nature of the salespeople often makes them easy to approach and talk to about competitors. Industry trade shows tend to be a rich resource for finding and making contacts among competitors within a given industry.

Customers

Customers are usually the most thoughtful and objective source of information about a company. In many instances, they can crystallize a large amount of information in a few sentences simply by answering the question of why they are doing business with that particular company. If the customers are unhappy or angry about how they are treated, that clearly tells you one thing. Conversely, if the customers are happy or generally pleased, that tells you another. Unfortunately, most of the time it is difficult to get a highly positive or negative response from a customer; however, it is possible to pick up a sense of their general feeling about the relationship.

Suppliers

Vendors and suppliers who sell products and services to the company are often especially knowledgeable about the company and the industry. In fact, when talking off the record, vendors and suppliers to an industry can often provide very useful insights into not just the company but the industry itself. Again, as in dealing with any related party, keeping information confidential and being honest about your assessments certainly help in developing these types of relationships.

Trade Associations

Trade associations can also be a valuable resource when researching a company. Of course, trade associations typically will not say negative things about their members; however, they may say telling things about companies that are not members of their trade associations. In addition, trade associations often have unique and aggregated data about a whole industry that is sometimes packaged and available for free or for a small cost on their web sites. It may be possible to arrange an introduction from the company to the trade association. This will help to open the door to the trade association and get a more meaningful response than you otherwise would obtain by contacting the trade association directly.

Industry Professionals

Industry professionals are also good contacts and can be useful resources. They are capable of making perceptive judgments about the company and the industry because of their special skills and because they see a lot of other companies that might be comparable to the company being researched.

Legal Documents

We live in a highly litigious society. The by-product of all the commercial litigation that goes on in the public arena is a massive amount of legal filings, which can be a useful source of information about a specific company or an industry in general. They can be difficult and laborious to read; however, such legal communications can yield a large amount of information. Information about the lawsuits themselves can often be discovered by reading the publicly filed disclosure documents of the company and then referencing them back to the state and federal courts that are the venues for the company. Pleadings and responses, as well as judicial opinions, can often be found as a matter of public record on the web sites of various courts.

PUBLIC COMPANY FEDERAL FILINGS

Material information must be made publicly available by companies so that all shareholders and potential shareholders can have equal and immediate access to material facts. Professional investment managers cannot by law have significant information made available to them that is not also made available to the general public. This concept of limited but equal access to public company information is usually termed "full and timely accurate public disclosure of material information." This basic principle can be the cornerstone of the information advantage discussed earlier in this book.

The officers of a company and the board of directors are required to review all information that is relevant to the company. Then they must decide what is material information and therefore must be made public. As has been in the news over the last few years, there's a great debate about what rises to the level of material information in choosing from the various methods of accurate presentation of financial and corporate information. Of course, the courts have become the final word on what is material and whether insiders have made the required disclosures.

Public companies are allowed to maintain confidential information from their shareholders because of the need to protect proprietary information and proprietary technology. Public disclosure of certain information could hurt a company's competitive advantage or position and, in conjunction, hurt the earnings power of the company. Members of the public, shareholders, and investment managers often believe that their questions deserve an answer; however, company officers often tell only a minimal amount of information in order to satisfy disclosure requirements.

There is adequate justification for company management to withhold key information, and the law recognizes that ability. However, if a company is not disclosing material facts as it goes along, shareholders have a legal remedy through suing the officers and directors for damages after the facts become public. These suits are seen more and more frequently as shareholder rights litigation becomes a growing area within the legal community. As a result, the important question is whether the withholding of such material information was in the best interest of the company or whether it was instead to try to hide problems within the company. At times, as we have seen, this nondisclosure of material information actually rises to the level of fraud and becomes a criminal act.

The issue of access to information is somewhat problematic in the micro cap sector. As a matter of business practice, there are many micro cap companies that make it very difficult for the public at large to obtain any significant material information about the company. Sometimes it is worth discussing with management the lack of information flow, but at other times it is more productive to move on to companies that welcome the interest of potential outside shareholders rather than fearing it.

Many companies provide a broad range of information that is readily available, both to shareholders and to the nonshareholding public. While other sources are very important, the company itself should not be overlooked as a significant potential source of meaningful information. Of course, companies will send basic financial information such as annual and quarterly reports and news releases as well as reprints of articles and speeches made by management to just about anyone who requests them from the company. Often, all this material is presented on the company's public web site and is easily downloadable from that web site. The company may be willing to send basic product literature and might also have public relations newsletters and regular marketing and sales material. You can usually be added to the distribution list, either via e-mail or regular mail, simply by asking the corporate investment relations officer. However, the most useful basic company information is often found at the Securities and Exchange Commission, and a simple Internet-based search will give an investor access to all recent filings and other useful public disclosures made by the company. Getting this information is relatively simple and inexpensive, and it can be done very quickly to gain a basic perspective on the company.

SEC REPORTS

Public companies are required to file a number of documents each year with the Securities and Exchange Commission in

Washington, D.C. These filings are required by statute to promote full and fair disclosure about company-level information. As a basic reference source, the following reports are worth reviewing to provide a meaningful overview of a company and its operations.

Annual Report Form 10-K

This filing discloses a good deal of information over and above what can be found in the written annual report of the company that is distributed to shareholders. It is really the foundation of the SEC's full and fair disclosure requirement and is normally the best single source of information available on a company and its operations. The SEC annual report 10-K should be available for all reporting companies. (This chapter discusses reporting and non-reporting companies in more detail later.) The information in the 10-K is required by federal regulations and is contained in two parts of the report. Part 1 must include the following 10 items:

1. An identification of the company's principal business and products or services, the principal markets and methods of distribution, and the material competitive factors surrounding the industry is required. This would include any backlog of work and expectations of the availability of critical raw materials as well as any important patents, licenses, or franchises the company may hold or grant. It also must describe the estimated cost of research and development, the number of people that the company employs, the effects of any new or pending environmental and regulatory issues, and any material litigation that the company may be involved in. If there is more than one principal business of the company, the company must describe for the last five fiscal years the revenue and net income for each principal business if it accounted for more than 10 percent of sales or 10 percent of pretax income.

2. A description of the company operations for each of the last five fiscal years and any additional years to assist in keeping the summary clear and accurate, as well as per-share earnings and dividends for those prior five years are required to be disclosed. Any change in accounting principles or practices must be disclosed, as well as the date of the accounting change and the reasons for the accounting change, along with its impact

on operating earnings and a description of that impact from the company's independent accounting firm.

3. The third section concerns properties, plant, and equipment. A listing of the location of the principal facilities of the company and any additional properties, leases, or significant capital assets are required to be described in this section of the report.

4. A list of all parent and subsidiary companies, and for each one named, the percentage of voting securities owned by the company that forms the basis for control must be described either in a narrative form or, for a larger, more complex organization, in the form of an organizational chart.

5. A description of material legal proceedings, including any pending litigation or any disputes that may result or are expected to result in material litigation, are required to be disclosed in this section.

6. Any increase or decrease in any outstanding securities, including information for each class of securities, is required to be disclosed in this section. The section will also account for reacquired securities and newly issued securities or securities that have been exchanged for property services or other securities, and the resulting valuation at the time of exchange. In addition, new securities that have resulted from a modification of outstanding securities such as a share split or distribution of securities owned by the corporation to shareholders must also be disclosed in this section.

7. A list of the holders of record for each class of equity securities as of the end of the fiscal year is required to be disclosed in this section.

8. A list of all corporate executive officers and the nature of family relationships between them and the positions and offices held must be disclosed in this section.

9. A statement of any arrangement and/or insurance under which any director or officer is indemnified or insured against any liability must be disclosed in this section, as well as the capacities and duties of each officer and director.

10. A list of all the financial statements as prepared by the company and reviewed by the company's independent auditors,

including all footnotes to the financial statements, must be exhibited as Section 10 of Part 1 of Form 10-K.

Part 2 of Form 10-K requires that five additional items be disclosed. Firms often meet this filing requirement by issuing a proxy statement for the annual meeting because these items are usually subject to periodic votes by shareholders or by the board of directors of the corporation.

1. This section identifies any owners of 10 percent or more of any class of securities and contains a listing of securities held by each of the officers and directors according to the amount and percentage of securities by class.

2. A listing of the names, offices, and terms of office for each of the directors and officers of the company must be included in this section. In addition, the biographical and business background of each officer and director must be included in this section.

3. A listing of the directors and the three highest-paid officers of the company, along with the aggregate total fees and remuneration paid to all officers and directors, must be listed in this section of the report.

4. Options granted to management and officers to purchase securities must be disclosed. This has been a topic of much debate in the past few years. The granting of options to officers and directors must be listed since the beginning of each fiscal year, along with a chart or table disclosing all the options granted to all officers and directors and the vesting price of those options.

5. In this section, a statement of material changes or significant transactions that may involve assets, pension, retirement, savings, or other similar arrangements, as well as loans to officers and directors, must be disclosed, along with the business interests of the related officer or director who will be benefiting from the transaction. Disclosure of certain material transactions can be very important for the analysis of conflicts of interest between the company and its management and outside directors.

Quarterly Report Form 10-Q

This report is required to be filed within 45 days of the end of each of the company's first three fiscal quarters. It is intended to be a quarterly update of the information contained in the annual report form 10-K. However, the information contained in Form 10-Q is slightly less detailed in its requirements than that in Form 10-K. The important difference is that the quarterly financial data are not required to be audited by the company's outside auditors. However, the regulations do require that management still provide a fair and accurate statement of results and also alert the reader to any significant special items that may affect the quarter or the ongoing business operations.

Material Current Events Form 8-K

This form is not filed on a regular basis, as Form 10-K and Form 10-Q are. However, this form is filed whenever a key event occurs at the corporate level. It often discloses material items not found in any other corporate filing. These data are especially important to small and micro cap companies because they may not be disclosed in any other venue outside of Form 8-K. There are 14 specific items that must be disclosed in Form 8-K:

1. Any change in control of the company
2. Material legal proceedings against the company
3. The acquisition or disposition of a significant amount of assets other than those that would occur in the normal course of business
4. The material withdrawal or substitution of any assets that may be securing any class of registered securities such as mortgage bonds
5. Changes in securities involving a material change to the rights of shareholders of any class of registered securities for any reason
6. An increase in the amount of securities outstanding if it exceeds 5 percent of the securities class outstanding

7. Default on any senior securities or debt obligations not covered within 30 days and affecting more than 5 percent of the company's assets

8. A decrease in the amount of securities outstanding that exceeds 5 percent of the total amount of securities outstanding

9. Options issued to purchase securities if the total amount exceeds 5 percent of the securities outstanding

10. The submission of any matters to a vote of shareholders

11. Any material extraordinary charges or credits related to any unusual material events including provisions for losses and any restatements of the capital or shareholders' equity account

12. A voluntary or involuntary change in the company's auditors

13. Any important event that the company believes to be material to its operations

14. Any changes or amendments in financial statements and exhibits that would support a previously filed corporate report, 10-K, or 10-Q

The key item to remember is that these SEC reports constitute an excellent source of information for an initial review of a micro cap company. After reviewing these forms, it is easy to decide whether you want to move on to secondary sources of investment information as described or if in general you have determined that the company would be of further interest. It is important to become familiar with these basic SEC reports and review them as a part of your due diligence process when looking at any new potential micro cap investment.

NOT ALL REPORTING IS EQUAL

Many micro cap stocks trade in the over-the-counter market and are quoted on OTC systems, such as the OTC Bulletin Board or the pink sheets. The OTCBB is an electronic quotation system that displays real-time quotes, last-sale prices, and volume information for many OTC securities that are not listed on the Nasdaq Stock Market or a national securities exchange. Brokers who subscribe to the system can use the OTCBB to look up prices or enter quotes for OTC securities. The NASD oversees the OTCBB, but the OTCBB is not part of the Nasdaq Stock Market.

The pink sheets are named for the color of paper on which they used to be printed. The pink sheets are not printed any longer, but rather are listings of price quotes for companies that trade in the OTC market, published on the Internet at pinksheets.com. Market makers are the brokers who commit to buying and selling the securities of OTC issuers. They can use the electronic pink sheets to publish bid and ask prices for micro cap stocks. A company named Pink Sheets LLC, formerly known as the National Quotation Bureau, publishes the pink sheets in both hard copy and electronic format.

As discussed, the biggest difference between a micro cap stock and other stocks is the amount of reliable, publicly available research about the company. Larger public companies file reports with the SEC that any investor can get for free from the SEC's web site. Professional stock analysts regularly research and write about larger public companies, and it's easy to get the current stock prices. In contrast, information about micro cap companies can be difficult to find due to lower reporting standards that result from the companies' micro cap size.

Companies that trade their stocks on major exchanges and in the Nasdaq Stock Market must meet minimum listing standards. For example, they must have minimum amounts of net assets and minimum numbers of shareholders. In contrast, companies on the OTCBB or the pink sheets do not have to meet any minimum standards. Federal securities laws require all but the smallest of public companies to file reports with the SEC. A company can become public in one of two ways: by issuing securities in an offering or transaction that is registered with the SEC or by registering the company and its outstanding securities with the SEC. Both types of registration trigger ongoing reporting obligations, meaning the company must file periodic reports that disclose important information to investors about its business, financial condition, and management.

This information is the first and best stop for micro cap investors. A public company must file reports with the SEC if it has 500 or more investors and $10 million or more in assets, or if it lists its securities on the following stock markets:

- American Stock Exchange
- Boston Stock Exchange
- Chicago Stock Exchange
- Cincinnati Stock Exchange
- Nasdaq Stock Market
- New York Stock Exchange
- Pacific Exchange
- Philadelphia Stock Exchange

In January 1999, the SEC approved an NASD rule allowing the NASD to require that all OTCBB companies file updated financial reports with the SEC or with their banking or insurance regulators. Beginning in June 2000, the rule applied to all companies on the OTCBB. Since then, any companies who have refused to file timely reports with the SEC or their banking or insurance regulators have been removed from the OTCBB or, in essence, are delisted from trading until the reports are filed.

When an OTCBB company fails to file its reports on time, the NASD adds a fifth letter "E" to its four-letter stock symbol. The company then has 30 days to file with the SEC or 60 days to file with its banking or insurance regulator. If it's still delinquent after the grace period, the company will be removed from the OTCBB. A list of securities that have been removed from the OTCBB is available on the Internet at www.otcbb.com.

With few exceptions, companies that file reports with the SEC must do so electronically using the SEC's EDGAR system. EDGAR stands for "Electronic Data Gathering and Retrieval." The EDGAR database is available on the SEC's web site at www.sec.gov. You will find all corporate filings in the EDGAR database, including annual and quarterly reports and registration statements. Any investor can access and download this information for free from the SEC's web site.

Smaller public companies with less than $10 million in assets generally do not have to file reports with the SEC. But some smaller companies, including micro cap companies, may choose voluntarily to register their securities with the SEC. As previously described, companies that register with the SEC must also file quarterly, annual, and other reports.

CHAPTER 7

Micro Cap Stocks and the U.S. Domestic Economy

This chapter will attempt to answer the following questions:

- Why are micro cap stocks more sensitive to the domestic economy?
- How do micro cap stock valuations compare to larger capitalization stocks?

An important characteristic of micro cap companies is the fact that they have relatively lower exposure than their big cap brethren to shifts in foreign economies. Sales of micro cap companies from foreign operations and exports account for on average approximately 18 percent of the total sales for micro cap companies. This compares with 35 percent of total sales from foreign and export sources for S&P companies. In addition, about 24 percent of micro cap companies report any foreign or export sales, whereas 69 percent of S&P companies report foreign sales.

The exposure to foreign markets can create a completely new dynamic within a company. Of course, the opportunity for growth in foreign markets can be substantial, but there is also a considerable risk involved in creating and running foreign operations. The most significant financial risk from foreign operations is that resulting from foreign currency exchange exposure. The translation of revenues from a foreign currency into U.S. dollars can have a negative impact on earnings, even though the foreign operation may be growing successfully. The variability of foreign exchange rates can cause large swings in a company's earnings, or the attempt to hedge foreign currency exposure can cause derivative financial product risk on the balance sheet. A rising dollar translates into lower earnings for a foreign operation; however, a foreign currency rising relative to the dollar can create an earnings windfall, boosting operating earnings of a company doing business in that rising currency. As mentioned, currency exposure can be hedged away on a short-term basis through the use of options and derivative currency swaps, and many large companies use currency hedging to smooth out foreign exchange exposure on an ongoing basis. However, it is important to note that there is an expense to hedging foreign exchange and that frictional cost can result in lower operating efficiency despite the currency hedging.

A strong and rising dollar can also put pricing pressure on U.S. companies. The relatively low exposure of micro cap companies to foreign markets can help reduce the risk of a strong and rising U.S. dollar. In addition, a falling dollar will have relatively little effect on most operations because they will not gain any foreign advantage as a result.

Beyond financial exposure, foreign operations can carry with them the political risk associated with operating in foreign countries. In many instances, the opportunity for companies to create and maintain foreign operations is most pronounced in developing and third-world countries. These very countries, while providing the largest opportunity, also create the largest potential political risk, as foreign governments and their policies can change dramatically in very short time periods. Companies with foreign operations, particularly those in emerging and third-world countries, must be concerned with the political and legal changes within those venues, and investors should also be very mindful of the political risks involved.

WHY MICRO CAP STOCKS APPEAR CHEAP RELATIVE TO LARGE STOCKS

Micro cap companies, particularly fast-growing micro cap companies, often have financial requirements that are different from those of larger companies in mature industries with established product lines. These differences can lead to some striking valuation differences between the financial ratios of micro cap stocks and those of their larger-company brethren. It is often most notable in the dividend policies of small versus large companies. Micro cap companies in general pay little or no dividends. It is estimated that only 26 percent of micro cap companies currently pay a dividend, compared with 88 percent of S&P 500 companies. In fact, dividends are even more prevalent among small cap companies as defined by the Russell 2000, where 49 percent of companies currently pay a dividend. In addition, the average yield among micro cap stocks is much smaller than the average yield among S&P stocks. For example, it is estimated that the average yield among micro cap stocks is currently 0.6 percent, while the current yield among S&P stocks is currently 1.4 percent—and that is compared during a period in which we see the S&P 500 current dividend yield being near all-time historical lows and valuations being at or near all-time historical highs, yet valuations still appear lower and dividends are currently higher than in the micro cap universe.

A closer examination of valuations within the micro cap universe will show that micro cap valuations tend to be clustered in one of two modes. There will be a group of micro cap stocks that trade at valuations that are significantly higher than the valuations of even the most expensive larger companies, and there will be a group of micro cap stocks that trade at valuations that are significantly lower than the aggregate valuations of their large cap relatives. The micro cap stocks that carry large relative valuations are typically early-stage development companies that have not yet realized their full earnings potential. These development-stage micro cap companies are often surrounded with great promise, and valuations can be surprisingly high given the modest financial position of many of these small companies. The Pozen Company case study discussed in Chapter 11 is an example of a development-stage micro cap company. As a result, the trailing price-to-earnings (P/E) valuations on these companies are usually much higher than the forward-looking P/E valuations of the expected future earnings.

Conversely, micro cap companies that either have fallen out of favor or are not in popular market sectors but rather in mundane businesses typically carry a lower valuation. These apparently cheap companies often have generated positive earnings over many years and in addition often create excellent positive cash flow. In many instances, these are truly value companies that can be bought at a significant discount in comparison to larger companies in similar businesses. As discussed earlier, many of these companies have little or no Wall Street coverage and have been overlooked by institutional investors because of their size. It's interesting to note that this bimodal distribution of valuation leaves very few companies in the average valuation range. It is important to understand this valuation distribution and to note the valuation disparity in the micro cap world. There are opportunities to be found in both these valuation pools. (See Figure 7.1.)

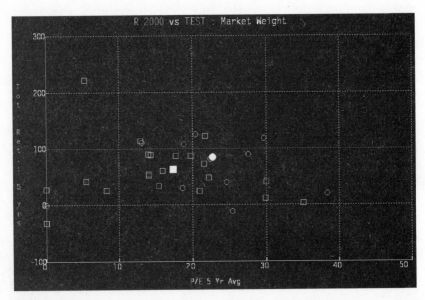

FIGURE 7.1 As can be seen in this scattergram, although the return profiles look relatively close, valuation as measured by average P/E is normally much lower for micro caps than for the Russell 2000 small cap index. The disparity only becomes larger as market capitalization increases.

Industry Analysis: Russell 2000 versus Microcaps
Market Cap Weighted Averages
SIC Code Classification

		P/E 5-Year Average
Totals:	Russell 2000	22.71
	Microcaps	17.43

INDUSTRY SUMMARY   **Russell 2000 versus Microcaps**

Industry	P/E 5-Year Average	Data as of 8/11/04 P/E 5-Year Average	Microcap P/E (–) Premium Microcap P/E Discount
ADVERTISING	23.98	10.32	57%
AEROSPACE/DEFENSE	22.75	17.09	25%
AGRICULTURAL PRODUCT	21.32	21.43	–1%
AIRFRGHT & LOGISTICS	31.52	15.67	50%
AIRLINES	11.74	13.63	–16%
ALUMINUM	6.69	20.27	–203%
APPAREL & ACCESSORY	14.8	19.1	–29%
APPLICATION SOFTWARE	53.47	48.95	8%
ASSET MANAGEMENT	12.22	8.28	32%
AUTO PARTS & EQUIP	23.9	10.97	54%
AUTOMOBILE MFRS	15.81	57.24	–262%
BIOTECHNOLOGY	9.87	5.98	39%
BREWERS	23.8	21.41	10%
BROADCASTING & CABLE	21.97	5.99	73%
BUILDING PRODUCTS	15.05	18.32	–22%
CASINOS & GAMING	27.41	11.89	57%
CHEMS-AGRI/FERTILIZR	41.4	13.19	68%
CHEMS-COMMODITY	32.46	39.55	–22%
CHEMS-DIVERSE	21.99	40.49	–84%
CHEMS-SPECIALTY	28.52	12.52	56%
COMMERCIAL PRINTING	24.32	46.19	–90%
COMMUNICATIONS EQUIP	45.38	24.39	46%
COMPU STORAGE/PERIPH	38.55	21.89	43%
COMPUTER HARDWARE	40.03	37.3	7%
CONSTRU & ENGINEER	17.66	16.75	5%

| | Data as of 8/11/04 | | Microcap P/E (–) Premium |
Industry	P/E 5-Year Average	P/E 5-Year Average	Microcap P/E Discount
CONSTRUCTION MATRLS	17.65	13.01	26%
CONSUMER ELECTRONICS	11.69	12.66	–8%
CONSUMER FINANCE	13.35	11.94	11%
CONTAIN METAL/GLASS	20.03	19.53	2%
DEPARTMENT STORES	7	11.11	–59%
DISTILLER & VINTNERS	15.1	28.28	–87%
DISTRIBUTORS	15.76	16.3	–3%
DIVERSE FIN'L SVC	13.88	24.62	–77%
DIVERSE METAL/MINING	19.66	16.24	17%
DIVERSIFIED BANKS	13.85	14.29	–3%
ELECTRIC UTILITIES	14.28	11.72	18%
ELECTRICAL COMPONENT	23.9	22.07	8%
ELECTRONIC EQUIPMENT	36.46	27.17	25%
ELECTRONIC MNFRG SVC	35.88	30.64	15%
FOOD DISTRIBUTORS	21.5	12.21	43%
FOOTWEAR	13.48	13.58	–1%
FOREST PRODUCTS	118.8	63.98	46%
GAS UTILITIES	23.65	18.2	23%
GENERAL MERCHANDISE	23.24	7.75	67%
GOLD	11.07	16.58	–50%
HC-DISTRIBUTORS	40.88	9.73	76%
HC-EQUIPMENT	32.45	25.26	22%
HC-FACILITY	21.08	11.93	43%
HC-MANAGED CARE	14.12	21.98	–56%
HC-SERVICES	23.84	19.45	18%
HC-SUPPLIES	21.35	30.18	–41%
HOME ENTMT SOFTWARE	14.17	11.75	17%
HOME FURNISHINGS	13.33	20.19	–51%
HOMEBUILDING	6.96	14.14	–103%
HOTEL/RESORT/CRUISE	7.05	9.76	–38%

| Industry | Data as of 8/11/04 | | Microcap P/E (–) Premium |
	P/E 5-Year Average	P/E 5-Year Average	Microcap P/E Discount
HOUSEHOLD APPLIANCES	27.2	21.96	19%
HOUSEHOLD PRODUCTS	16.25	25.91	–59%
HOUSEWARES & SPECS	15.54	14.49	7%
IND'L CONGLOMERATES	13.99	22.8	–63%
INDUSTRIAL GASES	17.7	32	–81%
INSURANCE-BROKERS	18.29	25.43	–39%
INSURANCE-LIFE/HLTH	12.21	22.13	–81%
INSURANCE-MULTI-LINE	14.25	14.87	–4%
INSURANCE-PROP/CAS	20.88	16.23	22%
INTEG TELECOM SVC	30.72	44.98	–46%
INTRNET SOFTWR & SVC	20.67	15.28	26%
INV BANK & BROKERAGE	10.96	11.87	–8%
IT CONSULTING & SVC	27.31	21.97	20%
LEISURE FACILITIES	32.08	10.78	66%
LEISURE PRODUCTS	16.25	15.92	2%
MACHINERY CONST/FARM	28.76	42.2	–47%
MACHINERY INDUSTRIAL	22.67	20.52	9%
MARINE	13.77	10.15	26%
MOVIES & ENTMT	8.88	19.72	–122%
MULTI-UTILITIES	15.4	1.44	91%
OIL & GAS-DRILLING	19.05	0	100%
OIL & GAS-EQUIP/SVC	48.43	56.75	–17%
OIL & GAS-EXPL/PROD	19.02	12.33	35%
OIL & GAS-INTEGRATED	18	19.58	–9%
OIL & GAS-REFNG/MKTG	38.87	11.57	70%
PACKAGED FOODS/MEATS	42.69	20.14	53%
PAPER PACKAGING	12.8	9.85	23%
PAPER PRODUCTS	20.58	25.09	–22%
PERSONAL PRODUCTS	23.85	17.99	25%
PHARMACEUTICALS	15.97	9.65	40%

| Industry | Data as of 8/11/04 | | Microcap P/E (–) Premium |
	P/E 5-Year Average	P/E 5-Year Average	Microcap P/E Discount
PHOTOGRAPHIC PRODS	107.4	84.86	21%
PUBLISHING	26.68	17.4	35%
RAILROADS	27.88	14.12	49%
REAL ESTATE INV TRST	9.16		100%
REGIONAL BANKS	15.03	14.99	0%
REITS EQ DIVERSE	6.92	7.86	–14%
REITS EQ HEALTHCARE	9	6.7	26%
REITS EQ IND/OFFICE	8.72	5.2	40%
REITS EQ RESIDENTIAL	10.13	9.48	6%
REITS EQ RETAIL	11.3	7.61	33%
REITS EQ SPEC/HOTELS	5.63	4.51	20%
REITS EQ SPECIALTY	9.59	7.23	25%
REITS HY HEALTH CARE	19.29	35.2	–82%
REITS HY IND/OFFICE	10.71	2.09	80%
REITS MORTGAGE BACK	6.53	4.42	32%
RESTAURANTS	21.36	16.01	25%
RETAIL-APPAREL	19.95	23.06	–16%
RETAIL-CATALOG	39.96	48.75	–22%
RETAIL-COMP/ELECTRN	8.64	15.59	–80%
RETAIL-DRUGS	18	23.52	–31%
RETAIL-FOOD	19.41	20.8	–7%
RETAIL-HOME IMPROVE	7.7	15.39	–100%
RETAIL-INTERNET	18.2	2.31	87%
SEMICONDUCTOR EQUIP	35.91	27.13	24%
SEMICONDUCTORS	56.3	43.91	22%
SERVICES-DATA PROC	20.24	20.98	–4%
SERVICES-DIV/COMM'L	20.88	20.1	4%
SERVICES-EMPLOYMENT	43.22	41.88	3%
SERVICES-ENVIRONMNTL	36.59	21.57	41%
SERVICES-OFFICE/SUPP	24.56	38.16	–55%

(Continued)

| Industry | Data as of 8/11/04 | | Microcap P/E (−) Premium |
	P/E 5-Year Average	P/E 5-Year Average	Microcap P/E Discount
SOFT DRINKS	26.77	28.28	−6%
SPECIALIZED FINANCE	13.53	19.16	−42%
SPECIALTY STORES	15.07	14.18	6%
STEEL	21.02	6.64	68%
SYSTEMS SOFTWARE	51.57	47.93	7%
TECHNOLOGY DISTRIB	18.84	23.14	−23%
THRIFTS&MORTGAGE FIN	11.3	8.87	22%
TIRES & RUBBER	7.15		100%
TOBACCO	11.82	6.5	45%
TRADE COS & DISTR	14.98	14.29	5%
TRUCKING	17.38	19.89	−14%
WATER UTILITIES	22.2	22.13	0%
WIRELSS TELECOM SVC	17.61	25.04	−42%

FUNDAMENTAL VALUATION TECHNIQUES FOR MICRO CAP STOCKS

When analyzing fundamental valuation ratios for micro cap stocks, it is important not to let any single factor summarily eliminate a stock from consideration. Because of the relatively dynamic financial nature of micro cap companies, there are reasons, at times, to discount some factors while putting more weight on other factors when reviewing the financial ratios of a company. For example, there are many rapidly growing small companies that generate very little free cash flow. Conversely, there are small companies that generate very modest earnings growth but generate significant levels of free cash flow from operations. Simple screening techniques could eliminate either of the companies from consideration; however, a little more effort within the analysis can yield potentially great stocks.

As is the case with financial ratios, certain measures will be more or less applicable, depending on the sector within which a company operates. It is often the best strategy to use ratios that reflect a company's valuation relative to its peers rather than relative to the market. In addition, it is important to study the accounting practices of the company and its peers to determine whether any adjustments are necessary for different accounting policies and procedures. For example, manufacturing companies tend to lend themselves better to cash flow and EBITDA (earnings before interest, taxes, depreciation, and amortization) analysis, whereas fast-growing service companies tend to better lend themselves to price-to-sales ratio analysis or earnings-per-share growth analysis.

BASIC FINANCIAL ANALYSIS OF MICRO CAP COMPANIES

Academic research as well as studies done by Uniplan Consulting, LLC, our financial research affiliate, have indicated that some screening variables are generally more useful for the purposes of finding micro cap opportunities than others. The intention here is not to do an exhaustive review of financial statement analysis; there are many excellent books on that topic, for example, *Financial Statement Analysis Workbook: Step-by-Step Exercises and Tests to Help You Master Financial Statement Analysis*, third edition, by Martin Fridson and Fernando Alvarez (Wiley, 2002). The goal is to review some relevant financial analysis techniques that will help micro cap investors screen out potential investment candidates from consideration for their portfolios.

As mentioned, the valuation criteria most suitable for a given micro cap company will depend largely on the type of business the company engages in and the value of the company relative to its industry peers. However, there are some financial indicators that are very useful in the screening of micro cap companies. Following are discussions of three simple valuation criteria including a description and some general comments on the strengths and weaknesses of each. We call them the "holy trinity" and use them as the basic screening tools to begin searches. Again, this is not meant to be an exhaustive list of valuation methods, but rather some general screening criteria that can help narrow the universe of micro cap companies into smaller groups for more rigorous analysis.

Price-to-Book Ratio

This is such a simple ratio that it is often completely ignored by the professional investment community. However, research indicates that a low price-to-book ratio is an excellent basic tool to use when screening for micro cap stocks. Generally, a price-to-book ratio of less than 1.5 to 1 is a useful level at which to begin screening. It is often a surprise to find that there might be a large group of companies that are trading at below book value. These companies are worth some study. Many have serious problems or potential problems. But in many cases routine screening can produce a list of financially healthy and growing companies with no obvious business problems that are trading at a market price below book value.

It is important to note that book value must be carefully studied when analyzing these opportunities. Tangible book value, sometimes referred to as *hard book*, is the book value after it is adjusted for intangible assets such as intellectual property or goodwill that may be listed on the balance sheet as an asset of the company. These intangible assets are often of little value outside the company or are very difficult to value with certainty, so in most cases it is best to exclude them from the book value calculation. When the adjusted book value after excluding intangible assets is near or below book value, then the company merits closer scrutiny. In many cases, these companies are simply out of favor or in industries that are not of current interest to the mainstream investment community. If that is the case, it may be possible to acquire shares at or below tangible book value. This normally provides the investor with famous value investors Graham and Dodd's "margin of safety" when buying a micro cap stock. In his later writings, Graham moderated his stance on the importance of buying companies at or below book value as a result of prevailing market conditions that translated into higher book value multiples. But in the micro cap world, there are frequently temporal opportunities to buy with a relatively good margin of safety.

It is not unusual to see entire industries that are out of favor or not of interest to the broader investment community show up in low price-to-book screens. The price-to-book screen works best with operating companies in more mundane businesses, such as the dairy industry, which is discussed in a case study later in this book. It is not as effective a screening tool for development-stage companies that have a high level of intangible or intellectual property on the balance sheet. These development-stage companies do lend themselves to a net cash analysis that functions for them in a similar way to book value for operating companies. The calculation takes current assets less all liabilities and relates this amount to the market price of the company shares. Sometimes it is possible to find a development-stage company that is trading at or near its net cash value. The question then becomes how does the future look for the company? An example of this is the Pozen Company, discussed in a case study later in this book. After the collapse of the Internet stock bubble, there were dozens of micro cap Internet companies that were trading at or below net cash value. However, most of those companies had a business model that burned some percentage of that cash each month and had little near-term hope of showing an operating profit. Those were not the companies to invest in at the time. Nevertheless, there were some that were nearing profitability and had this cash on hand. These were the opportunities in the then out-of-favor sector. Again, the thoughtful and patient micro cap investor saw many of those companies survive and produce extraordinary investment returns.

Price–to–Free Cash Flow Ratio

Take a low price-to-book company and couple it with a low price–to–free cash flow valuation, and the probability for investment success increases geometrically. It is important to note that the catalyst is free cash flow. There are many companies that trade at a relatively low multiple of cash flow, but have large debts and high structural costs that require the cash flow to sustain business operations. The company that has a high level of free cash flow, however, has the luxury of being in a position to impact shareholder value. In the most simple outcome, the company can declare its shares to be undervalued and use the free cash flow to buy back shares. This shrinks the shares outstanding and increases the profit per share for remaining shareholders. The company can deploy cash to perform any number of other actions to enhance shareholder value, including, as in the case study of Michael Foods in Chapter 9, using the cash flow to take the company private at a significantly higher share price. In the world of business, happiness is a high level of free cash flow.

Low Price-to-Earnings Ratio

It sounds very clichéd, but low P/E stocks in the micro cap world will ultimately be recognized. Many academic and investment studies point to low-P/E stocks as a powerful indicator of future stock performance. It is important to note that the low P/E in the micro cap world is the trailing or historic P/E. Because there is a general lack of analyst coverage of micro cap stocks, the ability to get a consensus forward earnings estimate is nearly impossible. Without direct guidance from the company, it is possible to estimate future earnings only by building a company financial model to estimate those earnings. This is not something the individual investor will typically undertake. However, finding companies that are trading at a low multiple of past earnings is a simple screen that can be used on most Internet stock screening sites. Again, because there are very few analysts that cover the micro cap world, these companies often post a strong change in earnings trend and trade at a low P/E multiple for some period of time before a broader cross section of investors realizes the valuation level and begins to examine the company. As can be seen in the Garan Company case study in Chapter 8, there are times that companies with good growth prospects and excellent business performance trade at low P/E multiples. This can be a window of opportunity to make excellent investments at reasonable prices.

CONCLUSION

In the micro cap world, stocks trading at a low price-to-book multiple, a low multiple of free cash flow, or a low trailing price-to-earnings ratio are the most likely to show outperformance over subsequent periods. If the investor can find micro cap companies that display all three of these valuation characteristics, they will have a high probability of investment outperformance. When these factors are coupled with positive insider activity, high-quality management teams, and smart-money recognition, the chances for excellent investment performance are simply a matter of time. The concluding chapters of this book present a series of case studies that examine companies that showed these characteristics and track the ultimate outcome of the companies and the investors.

CHAPTER 8

Micro Cap Case Study: A Company with All the Indicators

This chapter will attempt to answer the following questions:

- What does a typical micro cap opportunity look like?
- What are the indicators that suggest it is a good investment opportunity?

As Chapter 5 discussed, public company federal filings are a valuable resource for micro cap investors. One particularly useful group of federal filings related to a company but not filed by the company are those that are often referred to by the institutional investment community as *smart-money* filings. The SEC's Schedule 13-D, Form 13-F, and Schedule 13-G are called smart-money filings because under federal law they are required to be filed by wealthy individuals and large institutions. These institutions and individuals often have access to the best research and information available and have the deepest resources when it comes to making investment decisions.

Schedule 13-D is filed by any beneficial owner of 5 percent or more of any class of a company's stock. Form 13-F is a schedule that is required to be filed by investment management firms that are federally registered with the SEC and have at least $100 million under management. Schedule 13-G is filed by passive shareholders with a 5 percent or greater cumulative ownership of a company's shares.

The Schedule 13 forms are often very useful in finding investment opportunities that are of interest to large institutional investors or very sophisticated individual investors. It's important to note that not everybody who is required to file a Form 13 would necessarily provide outstanding investment results. But there have been a number of academic studies that show that smart-money filings, when taken as an investment portfolio, can often provide superior investment returns over time. For example, the legendary value investor, Warren Buffett, or his various corporate entities, often shows up as a form 13 filer at companies. These are not always micro cap companies; however, most people in the investment community would agree that if Warren Buffett is acquiring shares in a company, at a minimum it would be worth taking a look at the company. History shows that many companies in which Mr. Buffett has invested in the past have wound up being acquired or provided very substantial investment returns over long periods of time.

SMART-MONEY OWNERS

Garan (GAN) was a New York Stock Exchange–listed micro cap company that designed, manufactured, and sold apparel primarily for children. The company distributed children's clothing under the Garanimals name. Garan also distributed sports apparel such as T-shirts, knit shirts, and sweaters for men and boys under various trademarks and licenses the trademark Bobbie Brooks for girl's and women's apparel. The company sold its apparel to major department stores and national chains, with the largest amount of sales to Wal-Mart and J.C. Penney Company.

Cheap Valuation

The stock would have come through a number of various value screens during the year 2000; most notably, Garan was trading at below book value during the year 2000 and traded basically in a range from 80 percent of book value to about 1.1 times book value during the calendar year. This looked particularly cheap for a company that had a five-year historic growth rate of slightly over 20 percent. Although the company showed a slight earnings decline from the 1999 fiscal year to the 2000 fiscal year of approximately 7 percent, nonetheless, the company still earned $3.25 per share during 2000. (See Figure 8.1.) At the time, Garan had a market cap of approximately $100 million. In addition, the company traded in a price–to–cash flow range of four to seven times during the fiscal year 2000, a surprisingly low multiple of cash flow for a public company, particularly when you consider the fact that Garan had no long-term debt on its balance sheet. In addition, the company had an interesting history of paying special dividends each year. During 2000, the stated dividend rate was $.25 per quarter or $1.00 a year, which approximated a 4 percent to 5 percent dividend yield. At the end of 2000, the company paid an $.80-per-share special dividend, bringing the total dividend return on an annual basis up to nearly 9 percent based on the year's average share price for the company. By any typical valuation measures, this appeared to be a remarkably cheap company. (See Fig. 8.2.)

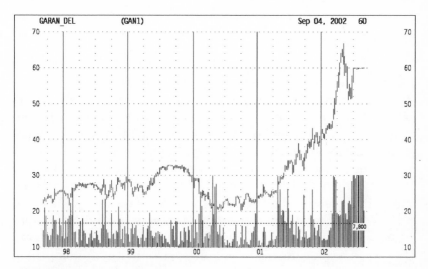

FIGURE 8.1   Garan price chart.

GAN1   **Garan Del**

Date	Rev (mm)	EPS	Yr/Yr % Chg Sales	EPS	Price	VALUATION P/E	P/S	P/B	ROE	Dividends	Shares Outstanding	Price Index	EPS Index
1991	147	2.03	-	-	19.38	9.5	0.7	1.3	14.0	1.10	5,018	100.0	100
1992	171	3.04	16.3%	49.8%	35.25	11.6	1.0	2.1	18.9	1.65	5,052	181.9	150
1993	190	3.32	11.1%	9.2%	32.75	9.9	0.9	1.8	18.8	1.80	5,070	169.0	164
1994	173	1.84	-8.9%	-44.6%	16.25	8.8	0.5	0.9	10.0	1.00	5,070	83.9	91
1995	141	1.08	-18.5%	-41.3%	16.88	15.6	0.6	0.9	5.7	1.00	5,070	87.1	53
1996	146	1.36	3.5%	25.9%	19.38	14.2	0.7	1.0	7.2	1.00	5,070	100.0	67
1997	153	1.92	4.8%	41.2%	25.75	13.4	0.9	1.3	10.1	1.20	5,070	132.9	95
1998	194	2.73	26.8%	42.2%	28.13	10.3	0.7	1.3	13.5	1.50	5,129	145.2	134
1999	229	3.49	18.0%	27.8%	28.63	8.2	0.7	1.3	15.9	1.80	5,306	147.7	172
2000	236	3.25	3.1%	-6.9%	23.38	7.2	0.5	1.0	14.0	1.80	5,072	120.6	160
2001	257	4.66	8.9%	43.4%	42.50	9.1	0.7	1.6	18.4	1.90	4,491	219.4	230

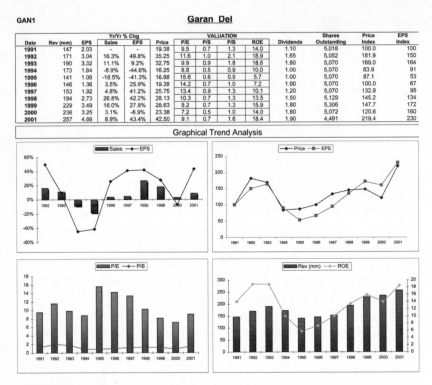

Graphical Trend Analysis

FIGURE 8.2   Historical valuation analysis.

Skin in the Game

A review of the proxy statement filed January 28, 2000, showed that company insiders owned just over 20 percent of the outstanding shares of the company. Of more interest was the listing of beneficial owners of over 5 percent not affiliated with the company. This list included Lord Abbott & Company, the well-known value managers from New York City; DePrince, Race and Zolo, a private investment company from Orlando, Florida; as well as Dimensional Fund Advisors and General Re Corporation, an affiliate of Berkshire Hathaway, Warren Buffett's company. Thus, we can see that Garan had a number of interesting indicators that could potentially signal an opportunity from an investment point of view. To begin with, the valuation level looked quite compelling relative to other micro cap companies as well to other companies in the garment business, both public and private. As discussed in prior chapters, a low multiple of cash flow affords companies a large amount of flexibility to withstand industry and economic downturn as well as to pay shareholders in several different ways. In the case of Garan, the management chose to elect special dividends from time to time as operating results created excess cash flow for the company. In particular, low multiples of cash flow in companies that have no debt or low levels of debt tend to create opportunities for management to distribute special dividends and/ or buy back company shares in the open market.

A relatively high level of insider ownership at Garan was also a positive indicator of a potential opportunity. Not only did company management own over 20 percent of the outstanding common stock, but for the previous 18 months they had been buying common shares in the open market. These insider purchases, as discussed in Chapter 5, are also possible indicators of future opportunities to come from a company or, at a minimum, an indication that valuation levels look quite reasonable.

Finally, there is evidence of excellent representation by long-term smart-money value investors in the company. With three major institutional investors owning over 5 percent of the outstanding common stock and management owning 20 percent of the outstanding common stock, analysis would suggest that, as a group, management and the outside shareholders would likely work closely together to create higher levels of shareholder value for the company.

This confluence of events presented an outstanding buying opportunity virtually any time during the year 2000, when the stock traded in a narrow price range from a low of approximately $20 to a high of approximately $25 for most of the year. During the year 2001, the share price moved from the mid-$20 range to over $40 in a steady progression of upward prices as the year went on. Share price of Garan rose very sharply during the first half of 2002, increasing from the low $40 range to over $60 per share in a very large increase in share volume. On or about May 17, Berkshire Hathaway announced a definitive agreement to acquire the entire company for $60 a share. Note that the Berkshire Hathaway affiliate, General Re, was a greater than 5 percent shareholder in the early filings of the company. On September 4, 2002, the transaction was completed and the company was taken over or acquired in total by Berkshire Hathaway for a cash purchase price

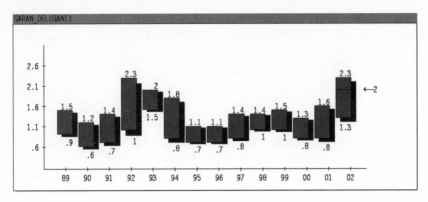

FIGURE 8.3   Price-to-book range.

of $60 a share. This stock had many of the correct indicators to be of interest to a patient micro cap investor looking for a long-term opportunity. (See Figure 8.3.)

An investment in the shares of the Garan common stock at the average price of $21.50 during 2000 would have bought an investment that had a stated yield of 4.8 percent. The special dividend that could be anticipated as a matter of company action during good years amounted to another 4 percent. This created a situation where investors were being, in effect, paid to wait while the market began to realize the intrinsic value of the Garan franchise. At the $60-per-share buyout value, the investment in Garan would have yielded a total return of 224 percent during the holding period of 29 months. It is the few Garan-type positions that typically propel the returns of a micro cap portfolio. Being invested and being patient are the keys to making the asset class work within a multiasset-class portfolio. It may never be possible to determine why or when a successful and well-managed company such as Garan might be sold. However, it's fair to say that the management teams of these micro cap companies are often frustrated with the share price available in the public market, and as discussed in Chapter 5, the principal agent theory might precipitate management action to maximize value in a single transaction. In the case of Garan it is difficult to determine, but it is worth reading the brief portion of the final proxy statement as filed on August 5, 2002, that describes the events leading up to the sale transaction. It has been edited here for length, with some comments added for background, but the primary events are well described.

The Transaction

From time to time over the last several years, Garan has been approached by investment banking professionals and others regarding the possibility of Garan engaging in a strategic transaction. Garan did not seriously entertain any of those proposals. In March 2002, Garan was approached by an investment banking representative of another apparel company regarding the possibility of a strategic transaction. Garan's senior management determined that they should meet with that third party, and following discussions with members of its board of directors, determined that it would be an appropriate time to engage advisors to consider Garan's strategic alternatives. (The rumor at the time of the transaction was that the suitor was VF Corporation, another, larger publicly traded apparel manufacturer.)

On April 3, 2002, Garan engaged Goldman Sachs to act as its financial advisor. On April 9, 2002, members of Garan's senior management met with representatives of Goldman Sachs, who presented an overview of strategic alternatives for Garan, including possible acquirors.

On April 11, 2002, representatives of Garan met with representatives of the apparel company that had expressed interest in the possibility of acquiring Garan. Shortly thereafter, representatives of that company notified Garan's CEO that it was not interested in pursuing a transaction with Garan.

Following discussions with other members of its board of directors, members of Garan's senior management decided to pursue the possibility of a strategic sale of Garan. (No one ever indicated why they decided to do this, but frustration over the low share price was rumored to be one of the factors.) At Garan's request, Goldman Sachs analyzed potential acquirors of Garan. Garan's senior management, after consultation with Goldman Sachs, determined that an open and widely marketed auction was not likely to maximize shareholder value. Garan's senior management also discussed with Goldman Sachs the advisability of conducting an auction process narrowly directed at a short list of more probable potential acquirors or approaching individually one or more of the most likely candidates, and determined they would prepare for the possibility of either approach. Goldman Sachs commenced a due diligence inquiry of Garan and the preparation of offering materials.

In late April and again in late May, Garan and Goldman Sachs were contacted by the investment banker who had originally suggested a strategic transaction in March 2002. That investment banker suggested that Garan consider a transaction with a different potential strategic acquiror and offered to arrange an introductory meeting. Garan indicated that it was not ready to entertain any inquiries, but that it would advise the investment banker if it was interested in a meeting.

Representatives of Garan (including six members of its board of directors) and Goldman Sachs met again in early June to review the process of analyzing Garan's strategic alternatives and potential acquirors. At that time, Garan's management and representatives of Goldman Sachs agreed that Berkshire Hathaway was the most likely and attractive potential acquiror. Representatives of Goldman Sachs advised Garan that Berkshire Hathaway, based on its past practice and public statements, would be unlikely to participate in an auction process and unlikely to be interested if not approached on an exclusive basis. Garan decided to have a representative of Goldman Sachs contact Warren Buffett, the chairman of Berkshire Hathaway, to determine whether Berkshire Hathaway would be interested in acquiring Garan at a specific price per share, which was in excess of $60.

On June 12, 2002, representatives of Goldman Sachs contacted Mr. Buffett regarding a potential strategic acquisition of Garan and the proposed price at which Garan would be interested in pursuing a transaction. The following day, Mr. Buffett advised Goldman Sachs that Berkshire Hathaway would be interested in pursuing an acquisition of Garan at $60 per share in cash, and requested that members of Garan's senior management meet with him at Berkshire Hathaway's headquarters the following week to discuss a possible transaction. Further conversations with Mr. Buffett confirmed that the $60 offer was firm and not negotiable. He also said that he would not be interested in Garan if other potential purchasers were contacted. In addition, Mr. Buffett expected the existing Garan management team to agree to remain with Garan after a transaction. On June 14, 2002, members of

Garan's senior management team met with representatives of Goldman Sachs and, following consultation with other directors, determined that they would be interested in a transaction with Berkshire Hathaway at $60 per share.

On June 17, 2002, Berkshire Hathaway executed a confidentiality agreement with Garan. During the afternoon of June 18, 2002, Seymour Lichtenstein, Garan's chairman and chief executive officer; Jerald Kamiel, president and chief operating officer; and William J. Wilson, vice president for finance and administration, met in Omaha, Nebraska, with Mr. Buffett to discuss the terms of a potential transaction. Mr. Buffett reiterated that he was interested in pursuing a transaction only if existing management agreed to remain with Garan and continue to run Garan, and that he expected that the existing employment agreements Garan had entered into with several members of senior management would be terminated in connection with the transaction. Mr. Buffett agreed that any change-of-control payments that would be due under those employment agreements would be paid out in connection with the transaction. Garan's senior management agreed in principle to recommend the proposed transaction to the other members of its board of directors, subject to the negotiation of definitive documentation.

On June 20, 2002, Berkshire Hathaway's lawyers delivered a draft merger agreement and stockholders agreement to Garan and its lawyers. Garan's lawyers prepared drafts of the amendments to the employment agreements of four senior Garan executives that would, among other things, terminate those employment agreements upon the closing of the transaction and provide cash retention payments to those executives in lieu of any change-of-control payments they otherwise would have been entitled to receive if they terminated their employment following consummation of the merger. An amendment to Garan's rights agreement was also prepared for the purpose of excepting the transaction from the rights agreement. The terms of these various agreements were negotiated over the course of the next 12 days.

On July 1, 2002, Garan convened a special meeting of the non-employee members of its board of directors to update them regarding the proposed transaction and the discussions with Berkshire Hathaway to date. Representatives of Goldman Sachs and Garan's lawyers (including Tannenbaum Dubin & Robinson,

LLP, general counsel to Garan; Hunton & Williams, Virginia counsel to Garan; and Simpson Thacher & Bartlett, special counsel to Garan) were present and led the discussion. Goldman Sachs advised the nonemployee directors of the progress of negotiations and the process by which Berkshire Hathaway was approached regarding a potential transaction. Goldman Sachs also discussed with the nonemployee directors other strategic options available to Garan. The nonemployee directors discussed with Goldman Sachs the likelihood that other likely potential acquirers would be interested in making a superior offer to acquire or merge with Garan. The nonemployee directors asked numerous questions relating to the process by which Berkshire Hathaway was approached and the possibility that any other potential acquirers could present Garan with an alternative transaction following the announcement of a transaction with Berkshire Hathaway.

In the early afternoon on July 2, 2002, the nonemployee members of the board of directors again met with Garan's lawyers. After discussion and questions, the nonemployee members of the board of directors determined that they were inclined to support approval of the transaction, subject to the discussion at the upcoming full board meeting.

Later in the afternoon of July 2, 2002, Garan convened a special meeting of its board of directors to consider approval of the acquisition of Garan by Berkshire Hathaway for $60 in cash per share. Garan's lawyers and Goldman Sachs were present. Garan's board of directors was advised of events relating to the transaction and the status of meetings of the nonemployee directors of Garan. Garan's lawyers advised Garan's board of directors of its legal duties in connection with the proposed transaction and reviewed with the board of directors the terms and conditions of the merger agreement, the stockholders agreement, the amendments to the employment agreements, and the amendment to Garan's rights agreement.

Representatives of Goldman Sachs then reviewed with Garan's board of directors Goldman Sachs's financial analyses with respect to the proposed transaction. Following this presentation, Goldman Sachs orally delivered its opinion to the board of directors of Garan, which was subsequently confirmed in writing to the effect that, based on and subject to the factors and assumptions set forth in its opinion, as of July 2, 2002, the $60 in cash per share to be received by the holders of Garan common stock pursuant to the merger agreement was fair, from a financial point of view, to those holders. After extensive discussion and deliberation and based on the factors described, Garan's board of directors unanimously determined that the merger agreement, the stockholders agreement, the merger, and the transactions contemplated thereby were fair to and in the best interests of Garan and its shareholders, approved and declared advisable the merger agreement, and resolved to recommend that the Garan shareholders vote to approve the merger agreement.

Following the special meeting of Garan's board of directors, the merger agreement, the stockholders agreement, the amendments to the employment agreements, and the rights agreement amendment were executed, and Garan and Berkshire Hathaway issued a joint press release publicly announcing the execution of the merger agreement and other agreements.

CHAPTER 9

Consolidating Industry Case Study

This chapter will attempt to answer the following questions:

- How can you take advantage of an industry consolidation through micro cap companies?
- What does a typical industry consolidation look like?

As discussed in Chapter 5, the consolidation of fragmented industries can be another powerful tool for finding micro cap opportunities. There are several different variations on the industry consolidation theme that can be played out in the micro cap arena. The most common consolidation strategy often focuses on a single acquiring company that has clearly stated its intention to consolidate a highly fragmented industry or industry segment by purchasing and consolidating a large number of smaller public and private companies into a single operating entity that can take advantage of the size and scale of a public operation as well as the lower cost of capital of a public company to create value for shareholders.

These types of fragmented industry consolidations often begin with the initial public offering of a relatively large company that has been created through a series of highly leveraged transactions to acquire a number of private operating entities to consolidate under a single public entity. Typically, the IPO transaction of this consolidating company takes the form of an equity offering to deleverage the private company and raise additional working capital for additional acquisitions. These industry consolidation IPOs can be attractive investments in and of themselves; however, they are often a powerful indicator of the early stages of an industry consolidation that can be played through the ownership of micro cap stocks within the same industry venue.

CASE STUDY OF SUIZA FOODS

One of the more interesting case studies in this area is that of Suiza Foods, which since 1996 has been in the process of consolidating the manufacture and distribution of fresh milk and related dairy products in the United States. In April 1996, Suiza Foods went public. Between the time of the company's formation in 1988 and its initial public offering, the company made 38 acquisitions in the fresh milk and dairy industry. Through these acquisitions, the company attempted to realize economies of scale and operating efficiencies by eliminating duplicate manufacturing, distribution, purchasing, and administrative operations. By the time of its public offering, the company had acquired a number of well-known private and public dairy companies including Suiza Brands of Puerto Rico, the initial acquisition; Velda Farms; Swiss Dairy Corporation; and Model Dairy. In its first Form 10-K annual report, the company stated its business strategy as follows: "The company's strategy is to continue to expand its dairy, ice cream and related food businesses primarily through the acquisition of dairy, ice cream and related food businesses in new markets and subsequent consolidating or add-on acquisitions in its existing markets. After entering new markets through acquisitions of strong regional operators, the company will pursue consolidating or add-on acquisitions where such opportunities exist. In addition, the company will seek to expand its existing operations by adding new customers, extending its product lines and securing distribution rights for additional brand and product lines." (See Figure 9.1.)

From its initial public offering, Suiza sounded the battle cry of an industry consolidation. Company management clearly articulated a business strategy that sought to take a highly fragmented,

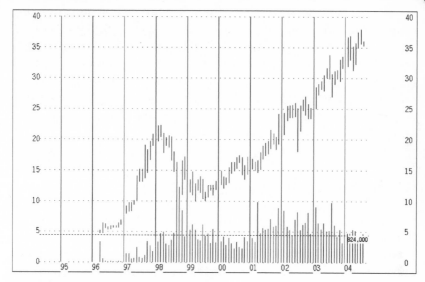

FIGURE 9.1   Suiza Foods price chart.

highly geographic-specific business—that of the production and distribution of milk—and consolidate it into a large-scale, centrally managed operating business that would take advantage of the efficiencies of scale that could be created by such an enterprise. In its initial public filing, the company put everybody who might be interested in reading the report on notice that it was in the market to acquire dairy companies and related businesses.

A review of the preliminary proxy statement filed in March 1997 would show a team of officers and directors that was built for the task of acquiring continuing operations. Gregg Engles, chairman of the board, was involved in and had been chairman of the board of Suiza Puerto Rico and had functioned in various other capacities since 1988. Mr. Engles had served as the president of Kaminski Engles Capital Corporation since 1988 as well and has been president of Engles Management Corporation since February 1993. Those two companies, with which Mr. Engles was directly involved, are investment banking and investment banking consulting firms, respectively. Mr. Engles was also president of Engles Capital Corporation, an investment banking and consulting firm, from May 1989 to October 1992. This is a very impressive resume for the chairman of the company, who in 1997 was 39 years old.

key members of the management team included
years as president and chief operating officer of Suiza.
_ars had been the CEO of Velda Farms, an acquisition
made by Suiza Foods in 1988. Prior to that, Mr. Beshears provided
consulting services to companies pursuing acquisitions of dairy
companies from 1980 through 1988. From 1965 to 1980, Mr.
Beshears had been president of the Southland Corporation and
chief operating officer of its dairy group.

A review of the balance of the officers and outside directors
of the company would show a virtual who's who of the investment banking and dairy industry, including Steven Green, managing director of GE Capital Corporation's Corporate Finance
Group; Tracy Knoll, former president of the Morningstar Dairy
Group; David Miller, former vice president of the board and chief
operating officer of J.C. Penney Corporation; and Robert Kaminski, president of Robert Kaminski Interests, a private investment
and investment banking consulting firm. Clearly, this was a formi-
dable management team that had access to public and private
capital markets and an outstanding history in consolidating the
dairy business.

With this now-public declaration of the company's intentions,
everyone was on notice that there were opportunities within the
dairy industry. During 1997, a quick search of the standard industrial classification (SIC) codes related to dairy and dairy products
would have included SIC code 2021, creamery and butter production; SIC 2022, natural and processed cheese; SIC 2023, dry and
condensed and evaporated milk products; SIC 2024, ice cream
and frozen dairy products; and SIC 2026, fluid milk. At the time,
there were 18 publicly traded companies within those industry
segment SIC codes, of which 11 were micro cap opportunities.

Among these micro cap companies, which at the time were
publicly traded, was a successful and growing national branded
product company called the Morningstar Group. Morningstar, at
the time, had a market capitalization of approximately $115 mil-
lion; in addition, the company had been growing sales at a rate of
about 15 percent per year for the previous five years and traded at
a P/E multiple of less than 12. The company had good primary
institutional research sponsorship with Donaldson, Lufkin and
Jenrette (DLJ) as a principal research and investment banking
sponsor. Analysis indicated that not only was this a well-run

public company in the dairy space, but it would also likely be the type of company that, due to its valuation and quality management team, would be of interest to a larger company attempting to consolidate the industry.

In June 1997, Suiza announced a definitive agreement to acquire Morningstar in a stock swap transaction for 12.6 million shares, or approximately $190 million, a 30 percent premium over where Morningstar had been trading prior to the announcement.

In its 1997 annual report, the company indicated that the dairy industry had excess capacity and had been in the process of consolidation for over a decade. Excess capacity was the result, in their opinion, of the development of more efficient manufacturing techniques, the establishment of captive dairy manufacturing operations by large grocery and retail chains, and relatively little growth in demand for fresh milk products. As the industry consolidated, many smaller dairy processors were eliminated and several large regional dairy processors emerged. According to published industry statistics, in 1995 there were approximately 651 fresh milk processing plants in the United States, a decline of approximately 50 percent from the 1,191 plants that were operating in 1982. The number of plants with 20 or more manufacturing employees declined from 792 to 447 over the same period. As a result of this consolidation trend, which Suiza believed would continue, the company believed it had favorable opportunities going forward to pursue additional acquisition opportunities.

The company continued acquiring public and private dairy operations. During 1997, Suiza acquired Country Fresh Dairy, a leading regional processor of milk, juice, and ice cream products based in Grand Rapids, Michigan, and Land-O-Sun Dairies, a Tennessee-based operator of fluid, dairy, and ice cream processing facilities in the southeastern United States. Those two acquisitions had combined sales of nearly $1 billion. During 1997, the company also embarked on a strategy to begin acquiring various companies involved in plastic packaging and packaged ice businesses. An observer of Suiza Foods at the time would likely have recognized the chance to study micro cap companies in the packaging and ice business to look for opportunities for additional micro cap acquisition targets.

As Suiza Foods continued to gobble up existing private and public companies in the dairy, ice, and packaging businesses, other smaller companies within the industry began to consolidate as well. In general, valuations began to rise across the dairy industry, as consolidation and acquisitions began to play out in the sector. At the same time, in July 1998, Horizon Organic Holding Corporation (HCOW), a producer of organic milk and branded refrigerated organic dairy products and juices, went public at an initial offering price of approximately $15 per share. The company marketed its products under the Horizon Organic and the Organic Cow of Vermont brand names in the United States, and Rachel's Organic brand name in the United Kingdom. It sold its products primarily through natural and organic retailers and regional conventional supermarket chains and mass merchants.

Shortly after the company went public, a review of a related Form 13-D showed Suiza Foods Corporation as the beneficial owner of 1.1 million voting shares of Horizon Organic common stock, or approximately 11.5 percent of the company's outstanding shares. The company had an initial market capitalization of approximately $175 million, putting it squarely in the micro cap arena. During 1999 and 2000, the company stumbled, missing earnings estimates in 1999 by a wide margin as well as showing a continued decline in earnings from $.14 per share to $.07 per share in the 1999-to-2000 fiscal year comparison. In addition, management took a $.21 per share restructuring charge during 1999 and an additional $.02 per share in 2000. (See Figure 9.2.)

Through all this disappointing operating performance, the company's share price sank from $15 to $5 per share by the end of the year 2000. During the year 2000, the company would have shown up frequently on simple valuation screens. In the first half of 2001, the company shares traded at or below book value for an extended period of time. In addition, during the same period of time, the company sold for a multiple of between 4.3 and 7.5 times cash flow. This was particularly cheap in consideration of the fact that the company had less than 10 percent long-term debt to total capital. With Suiza Foods being their single largest outstanding shareholder and a virtual who's who of value investors beginning to file Forms 13-D, this was another company that was displaying all the classic indications of a micro cap that was ripe for investment opportunity. (See Figure 9.3.)

It was no surprise that after the second restructuring charges, significant management changes were made. During that time

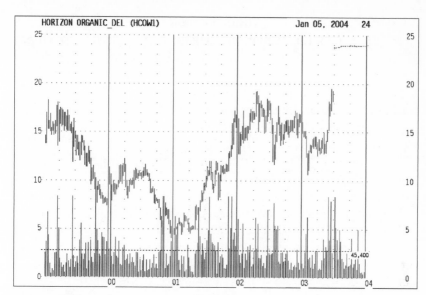

FIGURE 9.2 Horizon Organic price chart.

period, Lord Abbott & Company, the well-known New York value firm, had acquired 8.27 percent of the outstanding shares, and a large number of shares had been acquired and reported as owned by insiders at Suiza Foods as well as insiders at Horizon Organic—again, an indication that valuation had become cheap but business opportunities might be improving in the near future.

With regard to management changes, during the year 2000, Thomas Briggs joined the company as a new chief financial officer and treasurer. For the previous 10 years, Mr. Briggs had served as the chief financial officer for Denver-based Leprino Foods Company, the world's largest manufacturer of mozzarella cheese and one of the biggest private companies in the U.S. dairy industry. (In the interest of full disclosure, it should be made known that Uniplan managed investments for Leprino's profit-sharing plan during that time.) In addition, Clark Driftmier joined the company during the year 2000 as senior vice president of sales and marketing. During the previous 10 years, Mr. Driftmier served at Small Planet Foods, the parent company of Cascadian Farms and Muir Glen Foods, two leading organic food brands. Finally, Steven Jacobson joined the company in 2000 as vice president of operations. Mr. Jacobson had been a consultant with Denver

HCOW1 **Horizon Organic Del**

Date	Rev (mm)	EPS	Yr/Yr % Chg Sales	Yr/Yr % Chg EPS	Price	VALUATION P/E	VALUATION P/S	VALUATION P/B	VALUATION ROE	Dividends	Shares Outstanding	Price Index	EPS Index
1992	-	-	-	-	-	-	-	-	-	NA	-	-	-
1993	-	-	-	-	-	-	-	-	-	NA	-	-	-
1994	-	-	-	-	-	-	-	-	-	NA	-	-	-
1995	-	-	-	-	-	-	-	-	-	NA	-	-	-
1996	-	-	-	-	-	-	-	-	-	NA	-	-	-
1997	-	-	-	-	15.50	-	-	-	-	NA	-	-	-
1998	49	0.07	-	-	7.50	107.1	1.5	1.3	1.8	NA	9,656	-	-
1999	85	0.14	73.5%	100.0%	4.44	31.7	0.5	0.7	2.5	NA	9,744	-	-
2000	127	0.07	49.4%	-50.0%	16.52	236.0	1.3	2.8	0.9	NA	9,900	-	-
2001	159	0.17	25.2%	142.9%	16.19	95.2	1.0	2.7	2.9	NA	10,126	-	-
2002	188	0.34	18.2%	100.0%	23.95	70.4	1.3	3.8	5.7	NA	10,293	-	-

Graphical Trend Analysis

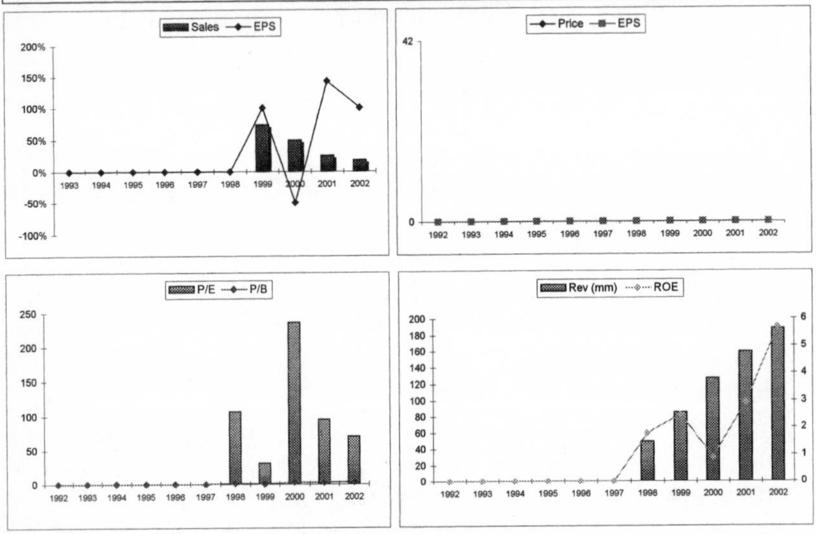

FIGURE 9.3 Historical valuation analysis.

Management Group, a consulting organization to the dairy and beverage industry, as well as having served as a distribution director for Medal Gold Dairies, a national milk processing and marketing company. With these key new employees in place, it appeared that the operating problems at the company were being addressed.

During 2001 the company earned $.017 per share with no special charges, and then during 2002 the company doubled earnings to $.34 per share, again with no special charges. The stock price exploded during that period from $5 a share to $15 a share by the end of 2002. In July 2003, Suiza Foods announced its intention to acquire Horizon Organic in a going-private transaction valued at $24 per share.

In an interesting and seemingly ironic climax to this case

study, during 2001 Suiza Foods announced its intention to acquire Dean Foods, the largest publicly traded dairy company behind Suiza and perhaps the most well-known name in the dairy space. On December 24, 2001, Suiza Foods completed its acquisition of Dean Foods and officially changed its name from Suiza Foods to Dean Foods, effectively disappearing into the dairy world as the leader in the dairy case, after consolidating most of the fragmented industry. Dean Foods, formerly Suiza, now has a market capitalization of approximately $6 billion and an enterprise value of $8.5 billion. During the fiscal year 2003, Suiza had revenues of over $9 billion and earned $2.27 per share. (See Figure 9.4.)

The company continues its growth-through-acquisition strategy. During 2003, it acquired another micro cap company, White Wave, Inc., for $189 million. White Wave, based in Boulder, Colorado, is a maker of soy milk and other soy-based products. Again, for a micro cap investor, Dean Foods' entry into the soy-based products area could offer some interesting clues for continued consolidation and acquisitions and opportunities as a micro cap investor.

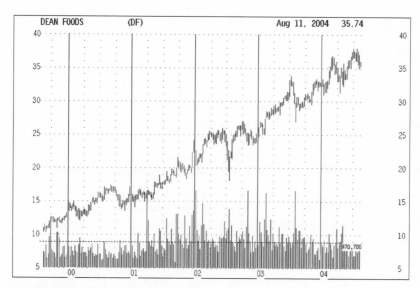

FIGURE 9.4 Dean Foods price chart.

OTHER OPPORTUNITIES

Another opportunity that arose out of the industry consolidation done by Suiza is the case study of Michael Foods of Minnesota. Michael Foods is a producer and distributor of food products. The company's primary business was the production and processing of eggs, which included extended-life liquid eggs, precooked frozen eggs, and other specialty products. The company's egg plants were fully integrated, housing nearly 13 million producing hens. In addition, Michael Foods processed and distributed a broad range of refrigerated products directly to supermarkets and these included cheese, butter, margarine, various muffins, juices, and bagels. Michael Foods also had a dairy products division that would process and sell soft-serve ice cream mix, regular ice cream, frozen yogurt mix, and other pasteurized milk products. Finally, the company had a potato products division that processed and distributed refrigerated potato products to the food service and retail grocery market. Because of the consolidation being undertaken by Suiza, Michael Foods would be of interest because a prudent investor might surmise that Michael might consider selling its dairy-related operations to Suiza in light of the continued industry consolidation.

Michael Foods typifies many of the conundrums faced by micro cap companies. Having gone public in 1986, it had an initial market capitalization of approximately $120 million. During the period from 1986 through 1996, the company traded in a narrow price range with a low of approximately $6 per share and a high of approximately $15 per share, with only a brief period during 1991 when the company's valuation exceeded that range. During that same time, the company had successfully grown sales at a compound average annual rate of 7 percent and had grown company earnings at a rate of nearly 12 percent per year. (See Figure 9.5.)

It's important to recall that a large percentage of the company was closely held by the Michael family. Their ultimate goal was to create a liquidity event and higher company valuations through the public markets. Since becoming a public company in 1986, the board of directors and management of Michael Foods, along with the Michael family, had set various goals in terms of sales growth and earnings growth in the hopes of enhancing shareholder value.

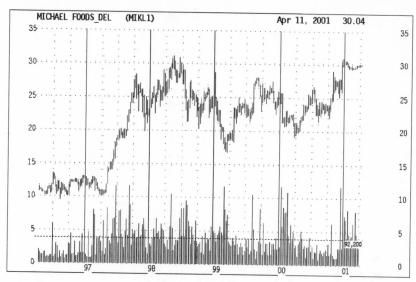

FIGURE 9.5   Michael Foods price chart.

Over that period, the board of directors and management generally felt that the publicly traded price of Michael Foods common
stock had not reflected the underlying value of Michael Foods,
the company. The company believed that a number of items had
adversely affected the value of the stock. These items included a
lack of investor appreciation for the value-added nature of its
business, the small market capitalization and small daily trading
volume of the stock, the inability to attract a sufficient number of
market makers and investment banking firms willing to prepare
research and analysis on the company, and the fact that directly
comparable companies against which institutional investors
could evaluate and analyze the performance of the company did
not exist.

In July 1999, the board of directors retained U.S. Bancorp,
Piper Jaffray, and Merrill Lynch as financial advisors to assist
them in evaluating strategic alternatives to enhance shareholder
value. Keep in mind that the Michael family, which was a large
percentage shareholder and interested in enhancing the valuation
of its holdings, primarily drove this process.

The board and management began to assess various alternatives related to the strategic plan of Michael Foods as a public company. The company looked at options such as generating growth

through strategic acquisitions, exploring the potential for a merger with a similar company, either public or private, of approximately equal size, and it also explored the possibility of seeking a sale of the company in its entirety to a strategic or financial buyer. The board of directors was particularly concerned that any strategic plan would result in a situation that could create sufficient growth to maintain and grow market position for Michael Foods in a consolidating industry, in particular fluid milk and the dairy section of the supermarket. If the company was to remain public, they felt they needed to achieve higher valuation through some combination of those alternatives. In this pronouncement from the board, which was made in numerous public filings, were the echoes of the overt pressures of Suiza consolidating the industry.

The company considered what would be the most common option for a small public company, and that would be to sell the entire company to a strategic or financial buyer. The board's desire to maximize shareholder value (possibly for the Michael family) was the primary consideration for a possible merger or sale. Board members considered the potential risk of attempting to continue executing the current business plan without any changes. They also considered the additional risk and potential benefits to shareholders associated with strategic acquisitions and enhanced internal growth. The board also felt that there was a lack of a compelling merger of equal candidates available in the public or private market. Finally, the board considered the possibility of strategic and financial buyers, particularly as this related to what was at the time a strong market for acquisitions that translated into good financing liquidity for financial buyers and higher business valuations at the time that were reflective of that liquidity and acquisition activity.

Ultimately, the board decided to ask its financial advisors to identify and contact potential strategic and financial buyers to solicit their interest in purchasing the company. According to the 2001 going-private memorandum, the company's investment bankers identified and contacted 61 potential acquirers to determine their interest in a possible transaction. Of those contacted, 32 parties were sufficiently interested to sign a confidentiality agreement and review a memorandum of offering regarding the company and its operations, which was prepared by company management in conjunction with its investment bankers. The result of that activity was that Michael Foods received preliminary expression of interest from six potential acquirers. Each of the expressions of interest included a preliminary evaluation for the company expressed as a range of price per share. The low end of the collective range was $28 per share and the high end was $35 per share.

After reviewing the preliminary expressions of interest with its advisors and management team, the board invited five of the potential acquirers to conduct further due diligence and refine their offers. The sixth potential acquirer, who was the low bidder, was offered an opportunity to increase the level of valuation, indicating that a minimum of $30 per share would be required to move forward. This acquirer declined to do so, and each of the five remaining potential acquirers conducted extensive due diligence and investigation of the company that included presentations by management and a thorough review of the financial performance and operating history of the company.

In November 1999, each of the acquirers declined to make a specific and final offer for the outstanding common stock of the Michael Foods Company, much to the surprise of management. Although not specific in their reasoning, the consensus among the potential acquirers was that the company would be fully valued at or near its then market price of approximately $26 per share. After receiving no definitive offers from the five potential acquirers, the board, through its investment bankers, contacted the sixth party that had submitted a preliminary expression of interest to the company. That potential acquirer, a publicly held diversified food products company, was invited to conduct due diligence on Michael Foods and its operations in order to refine its valuation for the company.

Over the next several weeks, the potential strategic acquirer conducted an extensive due diligence review of Michael Foods. During the same time, legal counsel and the investment bankers for the two companies began a discussion of the terms of a potential stock for stock transaction. A number of proposals and counterproposals were exchanged regarding an appropriate valuation ratio for Michael Foods and the potential acquirers' common stock. It is believed that this potential acquirer was Morningstar Foods, discussed earlier in this chapter in the Suiza Foods case study.

In January 2000, the potential acquirer made a final offer for the acquisition of the company to the Michael Foods board of directors. The acquirer proposed a fixed exchange ratio, and the market price for the potential acquirer's common stock at the time implied a valuation for Michael Foods common stock of slightly less than $28 per share. After extensive discussions with its financial advisors regarding the valuation and stock price data for the potential acquirer and the relative valuation data for both companies, Michael Foods' board of directors determined that the proposal transaction was not likely to provide shareholders with adequate value for their equity interest in the company. At that point, the board of directors terminated its discussion with the potential acquirer.

In January 2000, Michael Foods publicly announced that its board of directors had concluded a formal strategic review process without entering into any transactions. The stock price slowly sank to the $20-per-share price range. But the company indicated that the board might, without further public announcement, resume its formal strategic review process and would from time to time respond to follow-on opportunities created by those activities. Reading between the lines, the company made a public announcement to the marketplace indicating that it was available for sale and was looking for opportunities to have further discussions on that matter.

In June 2000, Greg Ostrander, chief executive officer of Michael Foods, along with a team of other members of management, began to seriously consider the possibility of a management-led buyout of the company. On June 6, 2000, Mr. Ostrander met with Jeffery Michael, a director of the company whose family and related parties beneficially owned approximately 17 percent of the company's common stock. Mr. Ostrander discussed with Mr. Michael and his family the possibility of the management-led buyout with the idea that the Michael family would possibly remain in some form as an investor in the company if it became privately held. Mr. Michael expressed a preliminary level of interest in continuing some form of investment in the company, depending on the circumstances. On July 17, 2000, Mr. Ostrander and Mr. Michael met with representatives of various banks to discuss the possibility of a management-led buyout of the company. During those meetings, bankers from Rabobank offered to introduce management to a number of financial sponsors who regularly participated in management-led buyout transactions. On July 19, Mr. Ostrander and other members of management retained a law firm to provide legal advice to him and members of the management group. On July 25, 2000, Mr. Michael, Mr. Ostrander, and the other members of the management team met with representatives of Banc of America Securities to discuss the feasibility of the management-led buyout and financing alternatives. By August, Mr. Ostrander thought he had enough potential financing interest in place to have a discussion with the board of directors indicating that he was involved in a preliminary exploration of the feasibility of a management-led buyout of the company. The consensus of the board was that Mr. Ostrander was authorized to proceed with an offer.

Throughout August and September 2000, Mr. Ostrander met with and had discussions with various private equity and capital firms to ascertain their level of interest in participating in a management-led buyout transaction. By the end of September, Mr. Ostrander decided to proceed with Vestar Capital and Goldner, Hawn, Johnson, and Morrison as coinvestors with the management team in the proposed transaction. During September and October 2000, the Vestar/Goldner group and its advisors conducted a due diligence review of the company and its business operations and held numerous meetings with financing sources, members of the management, and Mr. Michael in order to structure a preliminary proposal for the acquisition of the company.

During the week of October 30, 2000, Mr. Ostrander informed the Michael Foods board of directors and their lawyers that he expected to be in a position to make a proposal for the purchase of the company along with Vestar and Goldner at the board's regularly scheduled meeting on November 8 and 9, 2000. At the request of the board, Mr. Ostrander also informed representatives of U.S. Bancorp, Piper Jaffray, and Merrill Lynch of the transaction and requested that they be prepared to discuss the matter with the board during its meeting.

With the investment bankers now teed up, the company was in play. On November 3, 2000, Merrill Lynch was contacted by a senior executive from a privately held diversified agriculture and food company regarding that company's preliminary interest in discussing an acquisition of Michael Foods. Merrill Lynch had contacted this potential acquirer in 1999 as part of the board's formal review of alternatives to enhance shareholder value. After reviewing the confidential memorandum prepared by Michael Foods at the time, the potential acquirer had chosen not to pursue a transaction. Given its current interest, however, Merrill Lynch advised the executive to contact the law firm for Michael Foods, who, they understood, continued to represent the board of directors.

The executive contacted the attorneys and engaged in a discussion pointing to his company's preliminary interest in exploring an acquisition of Michael Foods. During the conversation, he reported that his company was considering joining with one of the private equity sponsors that had been introduced to Mr. Ostrander in making an offer for Michael Foods. The attorney informed the executive that the Michael Foods board of directors was not soliciting offers but would give careful consideration to any bona fide written proposal for a transaction that the potential strategic acquirer addressed to the board. The attorney also informed the executive that the Michael Foods board was scheduled to meet on November 8 and 9, and suggested that the potential strategic acquirer provide a written expression of interest in as definitive a form as possible to the board for consideration at that meeting.

The Michael Foods board of directors held a regularly scheduled meeting commencing during the evening of November 8 and continuing on November 9, 2000. Attorneys representing the board as well as investment banking representatives from U.S. Bancorp and Merrill Lynch attended the November 9 portion of the meeting, during which representatives of Merrill Lynch and the law firm and Mr. Ostrander reported their conversations with the potential strategic acquirer and its joint-venture partner and indicated that they anticipated that the board would receive an expression of interest from those entities during the board meeting.

Mr. Ostrander and representatives of Vestar and Goldner presented a written proposal to the board to acquire Michael Foods for a purchase price of $28.50 per share of Michael Foods common stock. During the presentation, the Vestar/Goldner investor group representative stated that substantially all of their due diligence was completed with the exception of certain environmental and regulatory matters. The investor group's written proposal included commitment letters from its lenders and a proposed form of the merger agreement. After the Vestar/Goldner investor group presentation, Jeffery Michael confirmed that he and various family members were equity participants in the transaction but that substantive terms of their involvement remained to be determined and no agreement as such to participate had been reached at the time. The board then met in executive session without Mr. Ostrander, Mr. Michael, or management executives of the company.

Legal counsel reviewed for the board the process that would be involved in evaluating and negotiating the proposal and the board's fiduciary duties and statutory obligations under the law, including the necessity of forming a committee of all disinterested directors to consider the proposal in order to meet the requirements of a public company. The board established the disinterested directors committee consisting of all directors who were neither participants in the proposal nor executives or employees of the company. After the committee of independent directors met, they concluded unanimously to continue to retain current counsel and current investment bankers as advisors to the independent committee of the board.

The investment bankers then reviewed for the board the process that the board had previously undertaken to evaluate strategic alternatives and updated certain valuation data regarding the company. The investment bankers informed the board that in their view the proposed offer price of $28.50 per share of Michael Foods common stock was inadequate. Although the board did not establish a valuation at which it would be prepared to sell the company, the consensus of the board was that it would not give serious consideration to any offer that valued the company below $30.00 per share. The board noted that the Vestar/Goldner investor group intended to obtain a portion of the debt financing necessary to acquire the company through the issuance and placement of a $200 million senior subordinated note, for which it had provided the board a highly confident letter from Banc of America Securities. The board and its financial advisors

THE MICRO CAP INVESTOR

considered the volatility in the high-yield debt market as a significant risk to the completion of the proposed transaction.

During the meeting, the board received by facsimile a written indication of interest from the potential strategic purchaser and its financial partner to acquire all the shares of Michael Foods common stock at $30 per share. The indication of interest stated that the valuation implied by the per-share price was based on publicly available information and might be increased if a due diligence review of the company's nonpublic records indicated that a greater value was warranted.

The board discussed a number of aspects of the potential transaction, including the possibility that it might be subject to time-consuming antitrust review, because the potential strategic purchaser and the company competed with each other in one of the company's core market segments. It was the consensus of the board that the potential strategic purchaser and its financial partner should be given a limited time to conduct due diligence and determine whether they were interested in making a more definitive proposal to acquire the company.

The board also decided that the Vestar/Goldner investor group should be informed that the board had received another offer of interest to acquire the company and that the board considered it sufficiently interesting to require investigation. The board viewed the Vestar/Goldner group proposal as financially inadequate and subject to unacceptable risk of consummation due to the lack of a firm financing commitment for $200 million in senior subordinated notes.

The board then discussed management's intention to provide the potential strategic acquirer and its financial partner with a two-week period of time to conduct due diligence on the company and refine its proposal and that board was requesting each group to provide it with their best final proposal by the end of the day on November 27, 2000.

Late in November, the Michael Foods special committee was informed that the potential strategic acquirer and its financial partner had been unable to reach agreement on several aspects of their proposed joint-venture arrangement and that the potential strategic acquirer was considering whether it wished to make a revised proposal by itself.

On November 27, the special committee received a revised proposal from the Vestar/Goldner group that valued the company at $30 per share. The proposal continued to include a highly confident letter that firm commitment for $200 million in financing senior subordinated debt necessary to consummate the transaction was in place. The financing commitments included with the revised Vestar proposal expired in accordance with their terms if not accepted on or before December 7, 2000.

On November 28, 2000, the potential strategic acquirer informed the special committee that it would decide whether it was prepared to pursue independently an acquisition of Michael Foods by the next day. Later that day, the board, with Mr. Ostrander and Mr. Michael recused, met and was informed of the revised Vestar/Goldner investor group proposal and the status of discussions with the potential strategic acquirer. On November 30, 2000, the potential strategic acquirer informed the special committee that the senior management of the strategic acquirer had a continuing interest in pursuing the acquisitions but that an additional two-week period would be required for the potential strategic acquirer to complete its due diligence and determine whether it was prepared to make a binding offer to acquire Michael Foods.

As part of its discussion with the independent committee, the strategic acquirer advised Michael Foods that its in-house legal counsel had indicated they did not expect any serious antitrust challenges related to the completed transaction, notwithstanding the two companies' competing core businesses. The committee requested that the potential strategic acquirer provide the board with a revised written expression of interest that included an indication of the upper end of its valuation range for the company based on its current due diligence to date.

Later in the day on November 29, 2000, the special committee received a letter from the potential strategic acquirer indicating that it continued to be interested in acquiring Michael Foods common stock at $30 per share and that its valuation for the company could increase to up to $32 per share depending on the results of a further due diligence investigation. The letter included a request for an additional two-week period to complete the process.

On November 30, 2000, the special committee met with its financial and legal advisors to discuss the two expressions of interest and formulate a recommendation to the Michael Foods board of directors. The special committee's financial advisors reviewed various matters for the committee including the very poor conditions in the high-yield financing market. The financial advisors also informed the special committee that in their view, based on their understanding of the investment parameters of private equity firms and experience in comparable transactions, it would be unlikely that the Vestar/Goldner group would be prepared to increase its offer above $30 per share.

The special committee also discussed the strengths and weaknesses of each of the two expressions of interest, including financing risk, antitrust risk, due diligence risk, and proposed pricing. After discussing a number of alternatives, including the possibility of rejecting both proposals, the special committee decided to recommend to the board that it consider either providing the potential strategic purchaser with a two-week period to conduct further due diligence in order to develop a more definitive proposal or providing the Vestar/Goldner investor group with a more limited period of time to revise its offer to include a higher price per share and fully committed financing.

Later on November 30, 2000, the board of directors, with Mr. Ostrander and Mr. Michael recused, met with its financial advisors and legal counsel. The special committee reviewed for the board the revisions to the Vestar/Goldner investor group proposal and the revised preliminary expression of interest from the potential strategic acquirer. The board discussed the matter, including the current market conditions for high-yield senior credit financing with the view that the Vestar/Goldner investor group was unlikely to be prepared to increase its proposal above $30 per share. After a thorough discussion of various alternatives, the board of directors unanimously decided to provide the potential strategic acquirer with a two-week period to conduct further due diligence in order to develop a more definitive proposal and, at the recommendation of their law firm, to engage special legal counsel to assist the special committee and the board in evaluating the antitrust risks associated with a transaction with the potential strategic acquirer.

The special committee recommended, and the board approved, that the potential strategic acquirer should not be permitted to access confidential information regarding the company's business in product segments in which the two companies compete until special antitrust counsel had an opportunity to assess and advise the special committee on the antitrust risk associated with the proposed transaction.

After the board of directors' meeting on November 30, the special committee informed the Vestar/Goldner investor group of the board's decision to continue to explore the proposal of the potential strategic acquirer over the next two weeks. The committee informed the Vestar/Goldner group that its proposed $30-per-share valuation and the lack of fully committed financing were significant factors in the board's decision not to proceed with exclusive negotiations with Vestar. The committee was informed that Vestar would not commit to extend its offer beyond December 7. Later that day, the special committee received a letter from the Vestar/Goldner investor group confirming that its offer would terminate at 5:00 P.M. on December 7, 2000.

The special committee retained a Washington, D.C., law firm to provide it with advice with respect to an antitrust analysis of the possible acquisition of Michael Foods by the potential strategic acquirer. Antitrust counsel in that office had previously provided advice to the company on related matters. From December 1 through December 7, 2000, Michael Foods' antitrust counsel and outside counsel to the potential strategic acquirer collected and exchanged relevant data about the two companies pursuant to the terms of a confidentiality agreement between the law firms that barred disclosure of the data to the firms' respective clients. During the same period, the potential strategic acquirer conducted its due diligence of the company. On December 4, Michael Foods' board of directors, with Mr. Ostrander and Mr. Michael recused, met by phone and was updated on the special committee and its legal counsel on the due diligence process of both companies.

On December 8, 2000, the special committee met with its legal counsel to hear and evaluate its antitrust counsel's analysis of the antitrust issues associated with the sale of the company to the potential strategic acquirer. After an extensive presentation by antitrust counsel, the special committee determined that the board of directors should have an opportunity to review the full presentation and conclusions of antitrust counsel. Later that day, the board of directors met, with Mr. Ostrander and Mr. Michael recused. After a brief summary of the antitrust counsel's presentation, at the special committee's recommendation, they decided to meet during the afternoon of December 11 for a full presentation and discussion of the antitrust analysis of the proposed transaction. On December 10, 2000, a representative of Vestar informed the special committee that Vestar anticipated making a revised proposal to the special committee on or about December 11, 2000. The Vestar/Goldner investor group delivered a revised proposal to the special committee to acquire the company for $30 per share, which included a commitment letter from Banc of America Securities and Banc of America Bridge Capital LLC with respect to both the senior secured credit facilities and the unsecured senior subordinated bridge notes. In the commitment letter, Banc of America Bridge Capital LLC committed, subject to the terms and conditions contained in the commitment letter, to purchase $200 million in unsecured senior subordinated bridge notes required to complete the financing of the proposed acquisition in the event that Michael Foods could not complete the private placement of the unsecured senior subordinated notes.

During the afternoon of December 11, 2000, the board of directors, with Mr. Ostrander and Mr. Michael recused, met in the offices of their legal counsel with their financial advisors. Antitrust counsel made an extensive presentation of the antitrust aspects of the possible acquisition of Michael Foods by the potential strategic acquirer. They discussed with the board the general review process of the Federal Trade Commission in a merger transaction and the various aspects of the transactions that often lead to a higher level of scrutiny by the FTC and various solutions to concerns that could be raised by the FTC. After significant discussions, the consensus of the board and its antitrust counsel was that there was a high probability that the proposed transaction would be carefully reviewed by the FTC and that the review process would extend over a number of months and would result in substantial expense to the company and greater uncertainty in the relationships of the company with its customers, suppliers, and employees and shareholders.

If the proposed transaction were challenged by the FTC, it would significantly increase the risk of completing the merger and related transactions. The board determined that the possibility of a transaction with the potential strategic acquirer, even at up to $32 per share, would be subject to an unacceptable risk that the transaction could not be consummated in a reasonable period of time at the negotiated price without substantial additional expense.

The board of directors then reviewed and discussed the Vestar/Goldner investor group's revised proposal with its financial and legal advisors. Legal counsel reviewed the terms of the proposed merger agreement and the financing commitments as well as other legal issues relating to the proposed transaction. Representatives of U.S. Bancorp Piper Jaffray advised the board that subject to internal procedures and a review of a definitive merger agreement, it would be prepared to deliver an opinion that the $30-per-share price for Michael Foods common stock to be received in the proposed transaction was fair to such shareholders from a financial point of view. Representatives of both U.S. Bancorp and Merrill Lynch indicated that they did not believe that the Vestar/Goldner investor group would be prepared to increase its purchase price for the company and advised the board that absent significant disruption in the financial and credit markets, there was a high degree of likelihood that the proposed transaction would be consummated. The special committee represented to the board of directors that the special committee and its legal counsel proceed to negotiate the terms of an agreement with the Vestar/Goldner investor group subject to final review by the special committee, disinterested directors, and the board. The board unanimously concurred with the recommendation of the special committee.

On December 13, 2000, representatives of the Michael Foods law firm provided the Vestar/Goldner investor group and its legal counsel with detailed comments on the proposed form of merger agreement. Representatives of the two law firms, with the active participation of the special committee, proceeded to negotiate the terms of a definitive agreement, and the Vestar/Goldner group and its advisors finalized their due diligence of regulatory and environmental matters. During these negotiations, among other things, the proposed purchase price was increased to $30.10 per share for the Michael Foods common stock.

During the same period, Mr. Ostrander and other members of company management participating in the investor group, representatives of their law firm, and representatives of Mr. Michael and other family members and affiliates and their legal counsel negotiated the terms of their participation in the transaction with Vestar. In connection with its proposal, the Vestar/Goldner investor group indicated that participation by company management and the Michael family and affiliates, as continuing investors, was a condition of its willingness to proceed. Vestar negotiated the terms and conditions of the continuing investors' participation directly with the investors, and neither the special committee nor the board took part in those negotiations. The special committee and the board viewed their roles as acting on behalf of the shareholders who would not be continuing investors. The special committee and the board did, however, review the proposed final terms of the continuing investors' participation to satisfy themselves that Vestar's condition was likely to be met and that the arrangements would not limit or otherwise preclude the board for effectively exercising its fiduciary duties or contractual rights under the merger agreement.

On December 15, 2000, Michael Foods' board of directors, with Mr. Ostrander and Mr. Michael recused, was updated by the special committee and its legal counsel and financial advisors on the status of the negotiations with Vestar and its due diligence process. The special committee and its legal counsel reported that significant progress had been made in narrowing the issues of disagreement in the proposed form of the merger agreement, although the drafting of precise terms remained to be completed. During the afternoon of December 21, the special committee, together with the full Michael Foods board, met with their legal and financial advisors to again consider the transaction. Representatives of their law firm reviewed with the special committee and the board the responsibilities and fiduciary obligations. US Bancorp Piper Jaffrey delivered its oral and written opinion that as of December 21, 2000, the consideration to be received in the merger by Michael Foods' shareholders, other than the continuing investors, was fair to such shareholders from a financial point of view. After a detailed discussion and analysis of the entire transaction and after receiving a recommendation of approval from the special committee, each member of the disinterested directors committee, and the full Michael Foods board, with and without Mr. Ostrander and Mr. Michael participating in the vote, unanimously determined that the terms of the merger agreement

were fair and in the best interests of the Michael Foods shareholders who would not be continuing investors, approved the
merger agreement and the transaction contemplated, and voted
to submit the merger agreement to a vote of the shareholders of
Michael Foods and to recommend that Michael Foods shareholders approve and adopt the merger agreement. In addition, the disinterested directors committee approved the participation of
Vestar and the continuing investors in the transactions related to
the merger. Later that evening, the merger agreement and the various agreements among the investors were executed, and Michael
Foods and Vestar issued a news release announcing the execution
of the merger agreement.

The Michael Foods going-private transaction in many ways
reflects the ongoing activities often seen among small public companies as well as larger private equity investors whose potential
strategic and financial position often brings them into the micro
cap arena for deal activities. In many ways, the Michael Foods
transaction is a textbook case study in the dynamics of a well-
functioning independent board of directors, the self-interest of
key executive management personnel, and large private shareholders, all culminating in a series of complex negotiations that
attempt to preserve the interest of all parties involved.

CHAPTER 10

Gehl Company
Case Study

This chapter will attempt to answer the following questions:

- What elements help identify a self-interested management?
- How do you spot when management is not acting in the best interest of shareholders?

Unlike Michael Foods, where management and other insiders had a large equity interest in the company, at the Gehl Company the chairman and CEO had very little financial interest in the company other than the nepotism of the family namesake and the ability to draw a large compensation package as a result.

The story begins in April 1999 at the corporate annual meeting of Gehl shareholders that was held in West Bend, Wisconsin. William Gehl, the great-grandson of the company's founders, was chairman and CEO of the company. He had taken over in 1992 and since then had led a successful turnaround of the financial operations of the Gehl Company, a small publicly traded manufacturer of farm equipment and construction machinery. In 1992, when Gehl took over the management of the family business, it was an overleveraged micro cap carrying a debt burden of $90 million, with sales of approximately $175 million. It had lost $18 million the year before and was in default on a number of its loans. In addition, the Gehl Company had not come out with a new product or modifications of any existing products for over six years.

William Gehl, who had been a successful securities lawyer and had worked on Wall Street in various legal functions, now came home to take over the family company, where he had been on the board of directors for five years. Gehl went to work immediately, cutting unprofitable business lines, mostly in slow-growth farm equipment, and streamlining the manufacturing process. He raised cash by selling excess inventory, closed out of several lines of business, and helped recruit distributors by convincing them that he could produce and deliver machinery better and faster than larger competitors. In addition, the company took tough action to collect past-due accounts and worked out a solution with lenders, convincing them that they would cover their debts while streamlining the number of suppliers they worked with and asking for a bigger financial commitment from their key suppliers.

In the sense of a micro cap company, it was a classic example of a new management team in place, taking actions to create shareholder value. During 1992 and 1993, the company shares could be purchased in a range of 30 percent to 70 percent of book value during most of the two years. In addition, the shares traded at 3.5 to 6.1 times cash flow during the same period. This was indeed cheap, but at the time, the future of the company was seriously in question as a result of the high levels of debt and poor operating performance. The catalyst of interest to the micro cap investor in this case would have been the new management team. Within a year, the company had completed a major refinancing at a lower cost, paid off old debts, and was nearing the break-even point on its operating business. This attracted the interest of a number of smart-money micro cap investors, including the Heartland Value Fund of Milwaukee, Wisconsin. (See Figure 10.1.)

In the meantime, the new management team was working hard to change the company's core business. When William Gehl took over, approximately 65 percent of the company's sales came from farm equipment, which was a mature market, growing at a slow rate, while dairy farms were consolidating into bigger operations that didn't buy as much of the equipment produced by Gehl. See the Suiza Foods case study in Chapter 9, for an overview of the dairy business. Again, here is the thread of the fluid

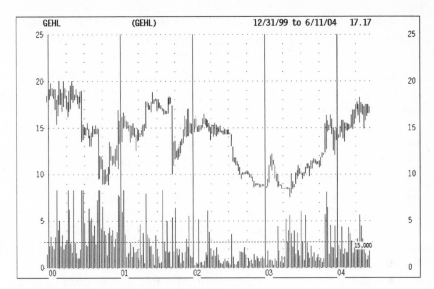

FIGURE 10.1 Gehl Company price chart.

milk industry consolidation and its impact on other companies, which ultimately created opportunity in the micro cap arena. (Note: See the Morningstar and Michael Foods Case Studies in Chapter 9.)

Company management had noticed that one line of business continued to outpace all others. The company was a manufacturer of skid loaders, which are essentially small, multipurpose farm and construction vehicles that can be outfitted with various attachments such as posthole diggers, loading buckets, backhoes, and forklifts. They typically sell as a package with other equipment for general contractors and larger farm operators.

Gehl Company had redesigned its skid loaders for the light construction business in the late 1980s and had enhanced its offering of skid loaders to the construction and farm sectors. The management team saw an opportunity, reasoning that as the economy rebounded and as construction activity increased, construction and landscaping companies would need a larger number of these versatile machines. In 1997, the Gehl Company bought Mustang Manufacturing Company, another maker of skid steers for the construction business. With the addition of Mustang, Gehl became the number four producer of skid loaders in North America.

The overall market for skid loaders grew strongly from about 6,000 units a year in 1990 to nearly 60,000 units a year in 1999. About 65 percent of Gehl Company's sales in 1999 now came from the construction equipment business, primarily in the form of skid-steer loaders. The Gehl Company hoped to continue expanding that line of business.

During the same period, as the Heartland Value Fund continued to accumulate shares, another smart-money shareholder showed up on the scene. James Dahl had quite a history in the financial service industry. Dahl was Michael Milken's leading bond salesman at Drexel Burnham Lambert during the junk bond era of the 1980s.

An outstanding account of that entire junk bond era was recounted in a book by James B. Stewart in 1991 entitled *Den of Thieves* (Simon & Schuster). In this book, Stewart indicates that Dahl realized in 1988 that Drexel's time was running out, as the government continued to investigate the practices of the company and increasingly focused on Michael Milken, the company's head. Dahl believed that Milken would, if given the opportunity, sacrifice any or all of his associates to save himself. As a result, Dahl became a government witness against Milken in exchange for immunity from prosecution. It's believed that without Dahl turning to the government, Milken would never have been convicted. Milken eventually pleaded guilty to numerous felonies as a result of Dahl's direct testimony. It is reported that Dahl left Drexel in 1990, after selling his stake in the company for $50 million.

Dahl now runs an investment advisory firm in Jacksonville, Florida, that invests in privately held companies and micro cap and small public companies that are overlooked by analysts. In the public market, he buys big positions in what he considers to be undervalued companies whose industry dynamics are changing. He then tries to work with management to boost share valuation and company performance.

During the first half of 1997, Dahl acquired a 5 percent stake in the company and on June 9, 1997, Dahl filed a Schedule 13-D, indicating an ownership interest in the Gehl Company of approximately 375,000 shares, or about 5.9 percent of the outstanding company stock. At around the same time, Heartland advisors filed notice of ownership of approximately 660,000 shares, or about 10.7 percent of the company. This compared to the executive officers of the company, who as a group owned less than 3.5 percent of the outstanding shares, with William Gehl personally owning approximately 2.3 percent of the outstanding common shares. As you might note, this is a management team that did not have much skin in the game, as investment bankers would say.

By the summer of 1999, Dahl had taken his stake in the company to above 10 percent. According to company filings and newspaper reports, as Dahl accumulated shares, he phoned Bill Gehl frequently. In most instances he tried to discuss merging, selling, or performing some other transaction that would increase the company's share price. In addition, he asked for a seat on the board of directors and was refused by Gehl.

As time went on, Dahl's advances continued to be rebuffed by the company. However, it appeared that the company was moving toward a position to be in play. With Dahl owning over 10 percent of the outstanding shares, Heartland Value Fund owning over 10 percent of the outstanding shares, and the appearance of Pioneering Management Corporation of Boston, Massachusetts, filing during 1997 a Form 13-G, indicating a 5.2 percent ownership stake, it suddenly was apparent that large institutional investors were becoming very interested in this small company.

In the meantime, Dahl got personal with Gehl. In a number of newspaper interviews, Dahl commented on William Gehl's inability or unwillingness to proceed with any actions that would enhance shareholder value. Dahl stated publicly that he felt the company should have been buying shares when they were as low as $12 in the spring of 1997, indicating that contracting (shrinking) the shareholder base at that time would have boosted earnings per share, potentially raising the stock price. In addition, Dahl criticized the company for failing to issue more shares when the stock hit $24 at a time when there were numerous potential acquisition opportunities and the company could have used the capital to enhance shareholder value and grow the company.

However, Dahl's biggest complaint publicly was that Gehl wasn't willing to listen to offers from other companies. Dahl believed that the giants of the construction industry were willing to buy all or part of the company. In public press accounts, he indicated that William Gehl flew to Tokyo to talk with Komatsu Limited, a large global manufacturer of construction equipment. He indicated that if William Gehl were a rational, clear-thinking businessman who had the interest of all shareholders in mind, he would understand that there were numerous large companies willing to pay high prices to acquire a position in this growth market. In newspaper accounts, Gehl acknowledges going to Japan, but would not discuss the details of whom he met with or why he took the trip.

In addition, a number of public research reports covering the Gehl Company pointed to the management's seeming lack of interest in increasing shareholder value. Some reports were critical of the compensation taken out of the company by the Gehl family. During 1996, William Gehl took out approximately $320,000 in salary and bonus. However, a careful reading of the company financial statements indicates that "the amounts for bonuses in 1996 do not include bonus amounts in excess of target which are credited to a bonus bank maintained for each of the named executive officers." Such bonus amounts in the bonus bank for each of the named executive officers are scheduled to be paid out over time but remain at risk and subject to loss pursuant to the company's shareholder value-added plan. This note indicated that an undisclosed amount of compensation was being withheld for the named officers of the company and, through various analyses, analysts believe that this may have been in amounts in excess of $1 million per year; however, the company was unwilling to disclose any amounts publicly that were credited to the bonus bank for management performance. This became a hot topic of discussion among analysts. The perception was that key officers, including William Gehl, were taking million-dollar pay packages while doing little or nothing to enhance shareholder value.

In addition, the analysts believed that the industry was changing. Most analysts argued that mergers between small companies that rented construction equipment would hurt the unit volume of small manufacturers of construction equipment like the Gehl Company. As these rental companies became larger, they would negotiate bigger and more significant discounts from the manufacturers of construction equipment. In addition, they provided easy venues for contractors to rent on a long- and short-term basis the equipment they needed to complete construction projects rather than buying it directly from distributors that represented companies such as Gehl. The net result was another changing micro cap industry environment.

Equipment rental companies like United Rentals, Hertz, and NES were gaining the clout to exercise more control over the entire construction equipment market. At the time, according to the Rental Equipment Register, an industry trade publication, the top 10 rental firms controlled over 30 percent of the construction equipment market. Another estimate at the time from John Lenz, a market analyst with Yangst Associates in Wilton, Connecticut, said that contractors were still the largest buyers of skid loaders at about 40 percent of the skid loader market; however, rental companies were close behind, with a 35 percent market share. At the time, about 7 percent of Gehl Company sales of equipment were directly to rental firms. As a note, this consolidation of the rental equipment market is just another case study demonstrating the potential opportunities in micro cap companies. Much like the Suiza case study in Chapter 9, this was another very public consolidation of an industry that was declared in public filings by a number of larger suitors.

Like Wal-Mart stores, the rental equipment giants were looking to acquire large quantities of low-cost equipment without regard for innovation or design uniqueness. This dynamic tended to favor the economies of scale enjoyed by the large, low-cost manufacturers who had big distribution and maintenance organizations in place to service the growing rental companies. In addition, skid load manufacturing companies that were competitors of Gehl were quickly being purchased by larger public machinery companies. For example, Ingersoll Rand Company, the giant conglomerate and one of the largest purchasers of raw material in the world, acquired Melroe Manufacturing Company, one of the main competitors of Gehl's skid loaders. With capital provided by Ingersoll Rand, Melroe expanded its manufacturing capacity for its industry-leading Bobcat line of steer loaders. To make matters worse for Gehl, Caterpillar and Deere companies, both large manufacturers of construction equipment, introduced their own lines of skid-steer loaders during 1997. An analysis of Gehl's financial statements indicated that skid-steers were Gehl's most important profit center, representing 44 percent of the company's total earnings. Analysts believed that with the expansion of the Bobcat line capacity in conjunction with Caterpillar's and Deere's introductions of new skid-steer loaders, a price war was about to break out in the marketplace.

In a growing series of management bungles, William Gehl announced publicly in the media that ". . . long-term, Gehl can compete with the biggest players. We've never shied away from competition." Among industry analysts, this was tantamount to burying your head in the sand. In a well-published report, a leading industry analyst commented that Gehl Company didn't have the superior product nor did it have patent protection and was competing against giants such as Caterpillar and Deere that had better access to financing, more distributorships, and deeper pockets. The large competitors could take losses in one segment as they squashed you in another, the analyst noted.

At the same time, right in Gehl's backyard of Wisconsin, there were two more major consolidations going on within the industry. At the time, Case Corporation, which had more than 23 times the sales of Gehl Company, was actively beginning a merger with New Holland to form the largest farm equipment company in the world. Both Case and New Holland were also major players in the construction equipment business and sellers of skid-steers. In addition, Omniquip International, a small publicly traded construction equipment maker based in Port Washington, Wisconsin, indicated that Textron Industries would buy the company for $477 million, or $21 a share—at the time, a 60 percent premium on Omniquip's $13 share price prior to the announcement. It was transactions like these, which could have easily been accomplished with the Gehl Company, that were endlessly frustrating the major shareholders of the company.

In what could be construed as the biggest slap in the face to other major shareholders, the Gehl Company bought out Dahl's stake in the company for $20.50 a share, or $14.9 million, a 10 percent premium on the trading price of the company at the time. In return, Dahl agreed not to buy Gehl Company shares for the next 10 years or talk about the company without William Gehl's permission. This self-serving treatment by management of one shareholder over another shareholder certainly raised the hackles of other large institutional owners in the company. The perception among large institutional shareholders was that William Gehl wasn't looking for someone to buy his company and was eliminating his largest public critic by paying greenmail to get rid of Dahl as a dissident shareholder.

On July 9, 1999, Heartland Value Fund sent a letter to William Gehl asking Gehl to appoint an outside director as the company's chairman and to form an independent committee that would help management review merger and sale proposals. The letter became public when it was filed with the Securities and Exchange Commission. In its filing, Heartland advisors indicated that the company was exercising its responsibility as an institutional investor and sent a letter to the Gehl Company communicating its views on two matters. First, they recommended that a committee of independent directors be created for the purpose of reviewing all and any proposals made to the company concerning any extraordinary corporate transactions such as a merger, reorganization, or liquidation involving the company or any of its subsidiaries or affiliates and the sale or transfer of a material amount of the assets of the company or any subsidiary of the company. In addition, it would review any strategic alliance between the company or subsidiary of the company and one or more other entities. Finally, Heartland advisors were recommending that the function of president and chief executive officer be separated from that of chairman of the board—currently, both functions were performed by one individual. Heartland believed that each function should be performed by a separate person, and Heartland had recommended that one of the company's current independent directors be named as chairman of the board and that the individual who currently performed both functions continue to serve as president and chief executive officer. That individual was William Gehl. Ironically, the Gehl Company announced that it would buy out Dahl just three hours after the letter from Heartland was filed with the SEC.

Gehl's transaction with Dahl left Heartland advisors and other major institutional shareholders holding the bag. They couldn't get the same deal from the company, and because they owned so many shares of this thinly traded security, they knew they couldn't get such a high price in the open market because a large volume of shareholder sales would have caused a severe drop in the share price. A number of institutional investors were understandably upset with this transaction. Several months before, a group of institutional shareholders had asked the Gehl Company to buy back a block of shares into the company's treasury at an average price of $18.00 to $19.50 per share. The Gehl Company had refused. The general consensus among institutional investors was that William Gehl played poker with Dahl and lost. Institutional investors would argue, understandably, that Gehl should have driven a harder bargain for the shareholders if, in fact, he had their interests in mind. And if Gehl really believed the company stock was undervalued and wanted to help shareholders make money, he would have found a buyer willing to pay what the company was actually worth.

As sad as it may be, the story of the Gehl Company's disservice to shareholders doesn't end with the Dahl transaction. By December 2000, there was another group of institutional investors that emerged as shareholders in a 13-D filing on the Gehl Company. In a letter to the Gehl Company and shareholders, two new entities, New Castle Focus Fund Limited Partnership and CIC Equity Partners Limited, disclosed that between April 2000 and November 2000 they had been purchasing shares of Gehl common stock in the belief that they were substantially undervalued. The parties behind New Castle Focus Fund and CIC Equity Partners were in principal Texas billionaire Harold Simmons and two of his executives, Mark Schwartz and Paul D. Rederobbio. On November 8, 2000, the group filed a Schedule 13-D with respect to its collective beneficial ownership of approximately 6.3 percent of the outstanding shares of Gehl.

On December 22, 2000, New Castle Partners and CIC proposed to acquire, through an appropriate acquisition entity to be formed, the outstanding capital stock of Gehl for $18.00 per share in cash, subject to standard conditions including completion of due diligence and obtaining all necessary financing. The offer represented a premium of approximately 67 percent over the then current market price of $10.75 per share. In a letter to the board, New Castle Partners stated that they continued to believe that there was significant value inherent in the company's business assets despite the Gehl board's failure to take any actions to attempt to maximize shareholder value. They stated that they believed the company needed to aggressively pursue strategic alternatives. To date, the board had not pursued such alternatives. Subject to a definitive agreement and normal due diligence, they offered $18.00 per share in cash for the company. Within four hours after New Castle delivered that letter to the Gehl Company, the board issued a press release summarily rejecting the offer.

In the press release, the company indicated that it intended to remain independent and would not have any discussion with any potential buyers. In a follow-up letter from New Castle pointing out that their offer would provide immediate liquidity to all of the company shareholders as well as a significant premium to the market price, they stated that the board's rejection of the offer, which was announced in a press release, indicated that the offer was not given serious consideration by the board. The offer was summarily rejected, with no indication that the board consulted with an investment banking firm or relied on a fairness opinion to justify the rejection. Instead of giving any consideration to the offer, it appeared that the board spent its time preparing a press release attempting to belittle the all-cash offer. Neither the board nor any representatives of the company ever made any attempt to directly contact New Castle or CIC.

On February 9, 2001, Heartland advisors, an entity that was unaffiliated with New Castle or CIC, again filing their amended Schedule 13-D, reported its beneficial ownership of approximately 6.1 percent of the outstanding shares of Gehl. It is widely acknowledged that Heartland was one of the principal sellers of stock to CIC, as is evidenced by its decline in ownership from 10.7 percent to 6.1 percent. Heartland advisors again sent a letter to each member of the Gehl board, dated February 8, 2001, which expressed Heartland's dismay with the Gehl board's failure to consider the interests of the shareholders by rejecting the New Castle offer and reiterating its previously expressed concerns over management's failure to engage independent advisors to explore strategic alternatives to enhance shareholder value. In the letter, Heartland advisors state that ". . . a board is elected to represent shareholders, not management. Both the board and management have a fiduciary responsibility to diligently and in good faith represent the shareholders. It is difficult to understand how the apparent cursory review of the CIC Equity Partners Limited offer can be construed as adequately discharging your responsibilities to shareholders. Your capricious actions have resulted in a shareholder lawsuit that will require company funds to defend and could result in further losses to the company. It is time you exercise your responsibilities to all shareholders. We urge you to appoint a committee of independent directors to promptly review the CIC proposal. We also reiterate our previous recommendation to engage professional advisors to assist the independent directors with respect to the proposed transactions and actions to return value to shareholders."

Again, it's interesting to see that company management at the moment decided to reject out of hand the desires of their largest shareholders. At the time, a number of lawsuits were being filed against the company based on fiduciary obligations of directors and disgruntled shareholders. Essentially now the company had opened itself up to liability from plaintiff's attorneys filing class action lawsuits against the company. The class action was filed on December 27, 2000, in the Circuit Court of the State of Wisconsin by a shareholder of the company. The complaint names the company and the directors of the company as defendants and alleges among other things that the company's directors breeched their respective fiduciary duties in refusing to discuss an offer from a third party to purchase the company. The complaint requests that the circuit court, among other things, declare the action a proper class action, instruct the directors to exercise their fiduciary duties, giving due consideration to any proposed business combination and/or to adequately ensure that no conflicts of interest exist between the directors and their fiduciary obligations, and award the costs and disbursements of the action, including reasonable attorney's fees and expert's fees.

As the legal and shareholder pressure mounted, the company began going through the motions as required by its legal obligations. On May 9, 2001, the company issued a press release indicating that it had retained a local investment banking firm to assist the board of directors in a review process to explore strategic alternatives and to maximize shareholder value.

In the press release, the company indicated that the board would evaluate proposals from U.S. and international entities. The board would compare the values that might be realized from various strategic alternatives to the long-term value it could expect to realize for shareholders from continuing to execute Gehl's strategic plan as an independent public company pursuing its growth strategies. Effectively, the company, with this press release, indicated that it would consider putting itself in play.

However, the language in the press release remained highly conditional and was predicated on a comparison of strategic alternatives as compared to pursuing its own growth strategies. Insiders close to the situation agree that the company had no intention of following through on any potential actions, but had to go through the motions to create a defense due to the litigation at hand.

By September 2001, the company announced what could now be considered a rather predictable outcome based on the prior actions of the management team. Issued on September 27, 2001, the press release indicated that the company unanimously determined that executing the company's strategic plan would create most value for shareholders. The company was to restructure to increase profitability, including an extensive revision of its manufacturing operations. In addition, the company announced an open-market repurchase of up to 500,000 shares of stock. There was nothing in the press release that indicated anything more about the company's actions with regard to maximizing shareholder value by accepting or reviewing offers other than that the CIC/New Castle offer was evaluated and rejected as a part of the company's strategic review.

But the story is certainly not over yet. On December 7, 2001, the New Castle group sold its interest in the Gehl Company to an Austrian manufacturer of construction equipment, Neuson Ag, for $20.00 a share, according to documents filed with the SEC. At the time, Neuson had a 12.9 percent stake in Gehl. When the transaction occurred, Gehl shares were selling at approximately $14.50 per share. After the announcement of the transactions, Gehl shares rose to $16.27 a share in trading volume that was three times the typical daily activity level. The transaction effectively ended the New Castle attempt to buy the company and to remove Gehl as the company's chairman and from the board of directors. In its most recent proxy filing of March 4, 2004, the Gehl Company listed Neuson Ag as a 14.4 percent shareholder. This makes them the largest single shareholder of common equity. As of May 28, 2004, the company's shares were trading at $16.90 in the open market. This is only 90 percent of book value and 7.5 times current cash flow. The market now seems to understand that this company should be priced at a substantial discount because management is not at all willing to act in the interest of shareholders. In addition, the market may be indicating that the

largest part of the skid-steer industry consolidation is over, and
the new dynamic will work against a small company like Gehl.
Gehl's shares continue to trade at a discount to the New Castle
cash offer and at a significant discount to the other offers
received in the past. The jury remains out as to whether the company will be able to successfully reposition itself and execute its
long-term business plan to add shareholder value, but it is clearly
indicative of a case where management put its interests ahead of
shareholder interests in an attempt to keep control of the company, although the managers had little or no financial interest in
the company at the time.

CHAPTER 11

Pozen Company Case Study

This chapter will attempt to answer the following questions:

- How do you identify development-stage companies with high potential?
- What issues should you consider when analyzing development-stage companies?

As discussed earlier in this book, there are opportunities in the micro cap arena to find companies that are emerging with new products and new services that are yet untested in the marketplace. These companies typically represent the highest-risk opportunities in the micro cap arena; however, they often present the highest-reward profile as well. In many instances, these are companies with products in the development pipeline that have a funding need to complete the creation and distribution of the proposed product. In most instances, venture capital has funded the critical early stages of the development process, and the company then requires a larger investment to complete the commercialization of the product or process. Although they are high risk, these deals should be considered for a small percentage of your micro cap portfolio.

It is interesting to note that when you look back historically, these companies and opportunities tend to appear in clusters with a generally similar set of circumstances. For example, during the late 1990s, many dot-com companies raised money through initial public offerings, some of which ascended to multi-billion-dollar market capitalization and others of which promptly collapsed and disappeared into the micro cap world. In many instances, it is possible to review the wreckage of these companies and find opportunities in real companies with real business models that are executing their business plans and are well-funded as a result of their public offering.

One area in particular where there are fairly consistent and ongoing offerings for development-stage companies is the pharmaceutical and biotechnology company arena. These companies often demonstrate the control of a new technology or a new pharmacological agent and require continuing funding for the development and distribution of the proposed new drug or product. These opportunities are interesting because after the fanfare and hype that surround the IPO subside, the newly public company often stumbles in some way, only to be completely abandoned by the mainstream analysts and investors on Wall Street. It is not unusual for such a company to turn into a micro cap company. If given time, management frequently has the opportunity to complete the execution of its business plan and move the valuation of the company to higher levels. It is important to note that not every company will successfully execute its business plan, and many will ultimately fail; however, if there is a good opportunity or if the company has a good product opportunity, finding a larger company to absorb it is normally the endgame for a small company like this when the business is not executing to plan.

An interesting example that fits this paradigm is the Pozen Company. Pozen, a pharmaceutical development company attempting to build a portfolio of products with commercial potential in targeted therapeutic areas, became a public company in October 2000. The initial area of focus for the company was migraine headaches, where they had built a portfolio of four potential products through a combination of compound mixing innovation and licensing. Their lead product, thought to have the most potential, was a development-stage drug created to be an oral first-line therapy for the treatment of migraine headaches. (See Figure 11.1.)

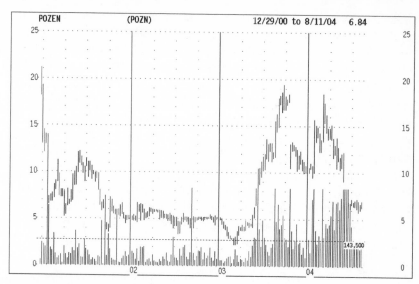

FIGURE 11.1 Pozen Company price chart.

As of September 2000, Pozen had completed Phase Three clinical trials of MT100, its oral therapy for migraines. At the time of its IPO, the company was conducting two additional Phase Three clinical trials, which were expected to be completed by the end of the year 2000. The company expected to begin Phase Three or Phase Two clinical trials for two additional migraine drug compound candidates in the first half of 2001.

As described in the IPO documents, migraine is characterized by recurring attacks of headache that are often accompanied by visual, auditory, and/or stomach disturbances. The typical migraine patient experiences attacks throughout his or her adult life. Migraine attacks vary in duration and severity, depending on the condition of the patient and the patient's environment. There are a variety of oral, injectable, and intranasal therapies that are currently available to treat migraine. The company estimated that the global sales of prescription pharmaceuticals for the treatment of migraine were approximately $2 billion in 2001.

Triptans are the family of drugs most commonly prescribed for the treatment of migraine attacks. According to industry statistics, triptans represented approximately $1.1 billion of sales in the United States in 1999 and were estimated to be $1.2 billion dollars of sales in 2000. Although triptans are effective in treating migraines, they have several significant side effects, including potentially dangerous cardiac events. Also, not all patients treated with triptans achieve pain relief from their migraine headaches.

MT100, Pozen's proprietary migraine drug candidate, combines a number of commercially available agents that relieve nausea, enhance gastric emptying, and act as anti-inflammatory and analgesic agents. The data from clinical trials on 2,250 patients who received MT100 in Phase Two and Phase Three analysis suggest that MT100 provides more rapid and sustained migraine pain relief than a placebo and as compared to the individual component compounds of MT100. Pozen also indicated that data from the trials on MT100 proved that the compound was as effective in treating migraines as Imitrex, the leading triptan in terms of U.S. sales. In addition, the company demonstrated that MT100, being generally well tolerated, also showed no indication of any serious cardiovascular side effects.

In its IPO, the company proposed to offer five million shares at a price of $15 per share to raise a total after fees and expenses of approximately $70 million. Upon completion of the offering, the company would have approximately 26.5 million shares outstanding. The prospectus pointed out that since its inception in 1996, the company had had no revenue and had incurred an accumulated deficit of approximately $34 million. The prospectus also pointed out that the biggest risks to the company were negative or unfavorable results from its drug trial programs and the possibility that even with favorable results, there was no certainty that it could obtain regulatory approval for its potential products.

However, a careful examination of the deal did indicate that there were a number of good factors related to the Pozen project. To begin with, 100 percent of the net capital raised, or approximately $70 million, was going directly to the company for the following purposes: About 65 percent of the funds would be used for the development, approval, and commercialization of new products; approximately 25 percent of the funds would be allocated to acquire products that are complementary to the company's in-process development product line; and approximately 10 percent of the funds would be used for general corporate and working capital purposes. The fact that all the net proceeds were going for corporate development purposes and no significant shareholders were cashing out on the IPO is normally a good indication of the long-term prospects for a company. After all, these shareholders had put up and spent over $40 million to get this company to the point of going public, and none of them were cashing out. Upon completion of the new equity offering, the company was estimated to have a pro forma net tangible book value per share of approximately $3.39. Prior to the offering date, the company had funded net proceeds through the private placement of preferred stock, resulting in aggregate total proceeds net to the company of approximately $39 million. As of June 30, 2000, the quarter end prior to the company's IPO, it retained cash in equivalence of $13.8 million on the balance sheet, available to fund operating activities.

At the time of the offering, the company had a total of 18 full-time employees, all based out of the headquarters in Chapel Hill, North Carolina. Of the 18 employees, 14 held advanced degrees and 6 had Ph.D. degrees in pharmacology. The company's management team read very much like a who's who of the pharmaceutical development, biotechnology, and pharmaceutical business community. The key officers and directors took reasonable salaries considering their broad industry experience and were compensated more heavily through the use of stock, which helped align their financial interests with those of the company. After the IPO, about 20 percent of the company would be owned primarily by management and approximately 28 percent of the company would be owned by three different equity venture capital funds that had participated in the initial funding of the drug development. In addition, the existing shareholders would agree to a lockup provision that prevented any of them from selling shares for the first 180 days after the date the company went public. In total, it looked like the company had a fairly good opportunity to successfully execute its public offering and to move forward with the continued development of the proposed pharmaceutical agents.

The company completed its IPO on October 13, 2000, at an offering price of $15.00 per share. By December 2000, the company's share price had reached an all-time high of $21.88. That's when the trouble began. In June 2001, the U.S. Food and Drug Administration (FDA) requested that the company conduct a two-year carcinogenicity study of the effects of MT100 in rats, prior to the approval of the MT100 new drug application. In the best-case scenario, this put the company two and a half years away from receiving approval, much further out than initially indicated by the original business plan. On June 26, 2001, Pozen submitted new data to the FDA in support of its request that the agency reconsider the need for the company to conduct the two-year carcinogenicity study. The new data consisted of genotoxicity study results and an expert report from two leading genotoxocologists. The company believed that the data would address the FDA's concerns about the genotoxic potential of MT100. The added time needed to complete the required study by the FDA caused the stock's price to decline sharply. Unfortunately, it was ultimately determined that the company would have to complete the required studies by the FDA for its MT100 drug, and the share price slumped to $5.00 by the end of 2002. Near the end of the first quarter of 2003, the company's shares experienced selling pressure as a number of institutional shareholders sold their holdings, and the stock price slumped to a range of $2.25 to $3.00 a share as the first quarter of 2003 ended.

During March 2003, a small window of opportunity opened, and an investor could acquire company shares at approximately 1.5 times the net tangible assets that were on the books. Those assets comprised primarily cash and cash equivalence and short-term cash investments. The intangible assets owned by the company were a series of patents related to Pozen's drug development activities, the value of which was carried at nominal valuation on the books and made it difficult to determine what real net value those intangible assets had.

During the second half of 2003, the company's prospects improved with a series of newsworthy events. In July, Pozen entered into an agreement with GlaxoSmithKline for the development and commercialization of proprietary combinations of triptan and long-acting, nonsteroid, anti-inflammatory drugs that may improve the effectiveness of acute treatment and provide substantial pain relief for migraine headaches. The announcement triggered a $25 million initial payment to Pozen by Glaxo-SmithKline and allowed the two companies to actively begin collaboration for clinical development and commercialization of relevant combinations of MT400, one of Pozen's development pipeline drugs.

In September 2003, Pozen announced the results of a Phase Three study demonstrating that its primary development drug, MT100, provided superior sustained pain relief over a placebo for patients in the early treatment of migraine. The data showed good efficacy relative to a placebo, with MT100 being administered as an oral, first-line therapy for the treatment of migraine headaches. Those two events helped push the stock price back up to nearly $18 per share by October 2003. Investors who had purchased shares in the $2 to $3 range in March of that year would have seen their stock price appreciate to the $16 to $18 range during August, September, and the early part of October 2003, a six- to ninefold increase in the share price.

On October 20, 2003, the company announced that its MT300 migraine treatment received a nonapprovable letter from the FDA. This caused the stock price to plunge, and by January 2004 the share price had declined by 50 percent and was trading at approximately $9 per share. On January 28, 2004, the company reported positive results from its MT100 migraine study, and again the share price moved higher; however, it was important to note that as the share price moved higher, a number of insiders moved quickly to sell a large percentage of their holdings into the strength in the stock, probably an indicator that valuation levels were abnormally high relative to the going-forward prospects for the company.

On June 1, 2004, the company announced that the FDA had issued a nonapproval letter concerning the new drug application for MT100, its primary product for the oral treatment of migraine headaches. In the letter from the FDA, the agency noted that Pozen demonstrated unambiguous, statistically significant superiority of MT100 compared to an appropriate control on a valid measure of pain as well as on three associated symptoms of nausea, photophobia, and phonophobia in one study. However, they noted that MT100 did not clearly meet these criteria in the second study. This disappointing news caused the stock price to plunge once again, and as we conclude this report, on June 18, 2004, the share price closed at $6.51, back to levels indicative of results in 2002.

The company's financial condition is beginning to deteriorate. Pozen currently has a cash burn rate of approximately $2.5 million per fiscal quarter or about $10 million a year. Based on its most recent fiscal quarter, which ended March 30, 2004, the company had cash in equivalence of approximately $56 million on the balance sheet. This would indicate that at the current rate, the company could exist for about five and a half more years before running out of cash. However, with the FDA's rejection of MT300 and the company's primary product, MT100, it is hard to envision how Pozen can recover through the development of new products. There may be some opportunity in the GlaxoSmithKline joint-venture development; however, that is in its early stages and it is difficult to make that determination.

There was a small window of opportunity to make a large return as an investor in this company. If one had purchased shares during the time period when they were trading at a low multiple of tangible book value and held onto them, pending several positive announcements, a large potential return might have been accomplished. It is important to note that at that time, Pozen was actively promoting the stock and discussing with potential investors the opportunities the company felt it had in going forward. However, it is easy to see how these companies are fraught with potential risk, and knowledgeable investors should study them carefully and attempt to determine appropriate entry and exit points when using them as part of their portfolios. In any development-stage company it is usually advisable to "take the seed money off the table," as is often said by micro cap investors. Thus, when a development-stage company doubles in price, selling back half the position and letting the gain remain invested is a popular risk control method.

CHAPTER 12

Private Investments in Public Equities (PIPEs)

This chapter will attempt to answer the following questions:

- What are PIPEs?
- How can they be used to find micro cap opportunities?

Private investments in public equities, also known as PIPEs, have dramatically changed the capital market landscape for small and micro cap companies. In addition, PIPEs are another excellent area of research for potential micro cap investments. A PIPE transaction is a negotiated private sale of a public issuer's equity or equity-related securities to institutional investors. The sale is conditioned upon a future public registration of the securities being filed, so they can be resold once they are declared effective with the SEC. This provides liquidity for resale of the private securities in the public markets once the registration statement becomes effective.

Because PIPEs are a private placement, they are regulated by the guidelines found in Section 4-2 of the Securities Act of 1933. This act provides an exemption from registration for the transaction of an issuer that does not involve a public offering of securities. This is the private investment side of the PIPE transaction. In addition, SEC Regulation D establishes a safe harbor for private offers and sales of securities that meet certain specific requirements when marketed to qualified investors. PIPE offerings are usually conducted using a Reg D qualified investor exemption. These are sophisticated investors who generally manage over $100 million for themselves or others.

In many ways, PIPEs are the bridge between the public and private capital markets. In most respects, they are structured like a private-venture capital equity investment; however, the investment is directed at a small or micro cap publicly traded company. In the past 10 years PIPEs have grown to become a useful and attractive source of capital for micro cap issuers, particularly during time periods when more conventional equity market financing in the form of public offerings may not be available due to market conditions. Because the investors who use PIPEs as a primary vehicle to invest in public companies are generally sophisticated, private-capital institutions, it is a sector that is certainly worth monitoring closely for opportunities in the micro cap investment arena.

The PIPE market as an investment vehicle for capital formation began approximately 20 years ago, when micro cap companies, which faced difficult financing constraints, were able to secure investment capital from private hedge fund investors and high-net-worth individuals and family offices. These were the type of sophisticated investors who qualified for the Reg D exemption.

In 1990, the SEC promulgated Regulation S, which allowed companies to sell unregistered securities to non-U.S. entities. It also allowed for these securities to be resold into the public markets after a 45-day holding period. Reg S allowed public companies to structure capital market transactions in the form of convertible preferred equity or convertible debt securities with multiple pricing features. Although these transactions sometimes hurt the valuation of the public equity of micro cap companies, they provided a valuable source of capital for small and micro cap companies.

During the 1990s, transaction sizes in the PIPE market using Reg S typically ranged from $1 million to $10 million, and the total size of the PIPE market grew from several hundred million dollars in the early 1990s to several billion dollars in the late 1990s.

By the late 1990s, the PIPE market began to take shape as a stable and viable capital market vehicle for small companies. During this time, more and larger companies began to take advantage of the ease and relative certainty of financing provided through PIPEs. Also, many micro cap biotechnology companies found additional ongoing financing via the use of PIPEs because of the difficulties of raising capital in the public equity markets. Development-stage pharmaceutical companies such as Pozen (see case study in Chapter 11) often used PIPE financing to continue product development through the raising of capital during periods when the public capital markets were less than favorable for them to issue equity.

In the past five years, the PIPE market has generally been legitimized among institutional investors. Since 1999, most large investment management firms, such as Fidelity, Putnam, and T. Rowe Price, have created investment affiliates that originate and invest in PIPE deals on behalf of their small and micro cap investors. It is estimated that private placements in public equities during 2001 and 2002, which excluded issuers with market capitalization of less than $25 million, had an approximate average transaction size of $20 million, and common equity represented the majority of PIPE deals during that time period.

PIPEs provide an excellent alternative financing vehicle for a small public company that may not find the current environment desirable for raising public equity in the capital markets. There are some key advantages for public companies when issuing or structuring PIPE financing:

- It offers greater flexibility in the tailoring of structure in terms of the offering.
- It allows the issuer to avoid the SEC registration process, permitting a faster time to market with regard to raising capital.
- Private and confidential capital raising is indicative of the PIPE structure, where no public filings are made until after the transaction is executed.
- Smaller transactions in the $5 to $25 million range are available at an effective cost to the issuer by avoiding the expense of the public registration process.
- The equity base can be expanded to strong institutional shareholders with long-term time horizons.
- It provides for access to capital when the public markets are not favorably positioned for raising equity.

- It allows micro cap companies that may be too small for any type of public offering to successfully issue equity or equity-linked capital.

As mentioned, PIPEs are typically offered through a Reg D private placement to a limited number of qualified institutional buyers. The growing number of mutual funds, investment advisors, private equity sponsors, hedge funds, and other financial institutions that now participate in the PIPE market have helped to broaden and deepen the size of the available capital pool for PIPEs. During the late 1990s and through 2002, typical issuers of PIPEs were companies in the technology, biotechnology, or pharmaceutical sectors looking for technology-based investment capital to continue executing a business plan. However, PIPEs have gained popularity across all industry sectors of the public capital markets, and now deals are common outside of the technology area. In the PIPE capital markets, the universe of potential investors is typically divided into two groups: fundamental investors and technical investors.

Fundamental investors are typically long-term equity investors who consider an investment in a company through PIPEs as they would consider any other equity investment. These fundamental investors tend to conduct extensive due diligence of the company over and above what is usual and customary through regulatory and SEC disclosures. Fundamental investors tend to have a longer time period for their investment horizon and typically will look out one to three years, or in some cases longer, when considering the opportunity to make an equity investment through a PIPE.

Technical investors, which would include hedge funds, convertible arbitrage funds, and certain venture capital funds, tend to take a more short- to intermediate-term view of their investment in a public company through PIPEs. In most instances, the technical investor is looking for some near-term catalyst to emerge that they feel will be perceived as beneficial by the public markets and as such propel share prices higher. Technical investors are more concerned about market and trading characteristics than fundamental investors. Share-price volatility and overall and total liquidity of an issuer's stock are of primary concern to the technical investor. Again, the time horizon varies but typically 6 to 24 months is the spectrum in which technical investors are looking at their investment horizon. In addition, hedge funds as technical investors typically manage the risk of their investment positions through using various hedging techniques to moderate volatility and lock in certain returns.

Although it is important to attempt to identify what type of investor has made a private investment in a public company, in order to determine the potential time horizon on which you, as a micro cap investor, may want to consider investing, it is becoming more and more routine to see syndicated PIPE deals that contain both fundamental and technical buyers of the same PIPE offering. And both fundamental and technical investors like to purchase PIPEs because they efficiently and seamlessly help them obtain a large position in a small, illiquid stock without having a large adverse impact on the market price. In addition, they allow them to leverage existing investment strategies and industry and sector expertise in smaller companies that may otherwise not present to them an investment opportunity.

Because of the liquidity constraints, the inefficiencies of the private market allow for negotiation and customization of terms that otherwise are not available in the public securities market. In most respects, these negotiated PIPE transactions represent the principal agent theory, discussed in Chapter 5, and they create a real and tangible pricing mechanism between the public and private securities markets.

TRACKING PIPE TRANSACTIONS

Regulation FD, which is now known as Reg FD, was enacted in 2000 in order to deal with the issue of selective disclosure of material nonpublic information by public issuers of securities. Reg FD was designed to create a level playing field between institutional and individual market participants. The fair disclosure rules of Reg FD prohibit a company from revealing material nonpublic information to selected investors without disclosing that same material to the public at the same time. While material nonpublic information does not have an exact definition under the regulations, most investment professionals would agree that corporate information can be viewed as material if there exists a substantial possibility that a reasonable investor would consider the information as important in making an investment decision. Information can be viewed as nonpublic if it has not been disseminated in a way that makes it available to all investors at the same time. Thus, a private placement of securities by an issuer in most instances would be a material fact.

Because the fair disclosure regulations would apply to public companies conducting any type of private offering, the information that companies are able to disclose to potential investors during the PIPE marketing process is restricted to publicly available information. However, through the use of confidentiality agreements, potential investors at times expressly agree to keep the information that the issuer is considering an equity offering in confidence until the transaction has been publicly announced or terminated. So a potential investor in a private investment offering for a public company would not be allowed to trade in the issuer's securities prior to such an announcement or termination of the offering. After a PIPE funding has been agreed to, the public issuer would be required by SEC guidelines and fair disclosure regulations to publicly disclose the transaction. Typically, an issuer would file a current report Form 8-K and issue a press release regarding the funding. It is the Form 8-K filings and press releases that provide a fertile opportunity for micro cap investors to discover potential candidates in the micro cap arena. This is a very useful screening technique when looking at micro cap opportunities.

As discussed in Chapter 5, private investments in public equities would be considered smart-money transactions. The investment professionals who are in a position to make a large private investment in a public company will typically have extensive industry and investment knowledge and will see there an opportunity that may not be apparent to the broader equity markets. In addition, because these investors may have a limited time frame, particularly in the case of technical investors, it is possible to construct a series of logical assumptions that would lead to an end point or exit strategy for a typical PIPE investor. There are several good venues for obtaining information on PIPES and private equity deals. Of course, the SEC, in its daily filing reports, would allow an investor to download and review all 8-Ks filed by public companies. Although this is a cumbersome process, investors who monitor such activity on a daily basis become fairly efficient at weeding through 8-K filings. However, there are several private databases available via the Internet that provide information about equity private placements. PrivateRaise.com is a web site that compiles statistics about private investments in public equities. The transactions on the web site are contained in a database that includes Rule 144A PIPE transactions, registered direct PIPE transactions, and non–rule 144A transactions. The database also documents the issuance of any equity or equity-linked security of over $1 million in nominal value that has been executed by a public company domiciled in the United States or public foreign-based company that has its primary trading listing or a significant trading presence on any of the U.S. stock markets. Equity and equity-linked security-type structures included in the database are common stock, convertible preferred stock, nonconvertible preferred stock that has warrants attached for common stock, convertible debt and nonconvertible debt with warrants attached for common stock, prepaid warrants, and equity lines of credit. This is a useful resource if you are going to seriously consider a focus on PIPE transactions as part of the micro cap screening process.

A BRIEF CASE STUDY OF A PIPE TRANSACTION: Ptek HOLDINGS

Ptek Holdings is a global provider of business communication services to large and medium-sized corporate customers. The company has two business units, Premier Conferencing and Xpedite. Premier Conferencing offers a variety of conferencing and Web-based data collaboration services, and Xpedite offers enhanced electronic messaging through various distribution channels including e-mail, fax, wireless, and voice. The company has a global presence and an established customer base of over 32,000 corporate accounts, including a majority of the Fortune 500 firms, spanning virtually every industry group.

A large number of businesses rely on data, audio, and web conferencing or electronic transactional messaging to manage a wide variety of important communications. The growth of these communication technologies and the increasing complexity of service requirements have created a large market for companies that wish to outsource these group communication processes. In addition, the current geopolitical climate coupled with corporate cost-cutting trends have encouraged companies to replace business travel with more convenient, reliable, and economical communications such as teleconferencing and videoconferencing.

Ptek went public in 1996 at $25.00 per share. The company had $52 million in revenue and was marginally profitable during its first year of operation. The company began a rapid expansion program in 1997 that included deploying a large number of assets into fixed infrastructure in order to accommodate the growing volume of conferencing activities. In addition, the company made a number of acquisitions of smaller enterprises and quickly grew sales from $52 million in 1996 to a peak of $458 million in 1999. However, the company was not able to execute this growth strategy at a profit. On a per-share basis, the company lost $.78 in 1997, $1.67 in 1998, $.72 in 1999, and $1.22 in 2000 as sales declined to $423 million in 2001. As a result of write-downs and charge-offs as well as continuing losses on its operating business, the company reported a loss of $4.84 per share. Although the company was largely unprofitable on a generally accepted accounting principle (GAAP) earnings basis, between 1998 and 2001 the company generated large internal cash flow through depreciation and amortization of capital equipment. So, although the company had had significant GAAP earnings losses, it managed to generally break even and even create positive cash flow during the period through 2001. (See Figure 12.1.)

During 2001 and 2002, the company presented what seemed to be an interesting investment opportunity. Sales had stabilized at around $425 million and the company was trading at a relatively low multiple of book value as well as a low multiple of cash flow. In fact, during 2000, 2001, and 2002, the company traded in a range as low as 1.0 times cash flow and as high as 6.4 times cash flow. On a cash flow basis, this was an extremely cheap company. Furthermore, in 2002 the company had created a stable EBITDA margin of 17.5 percent and a net profit margin of 4.2 percent, which created a return on equity of 17.7 percent. All these financial metrics suggested that if the company could continue growing, it would present a fairly attractive investment opportunity

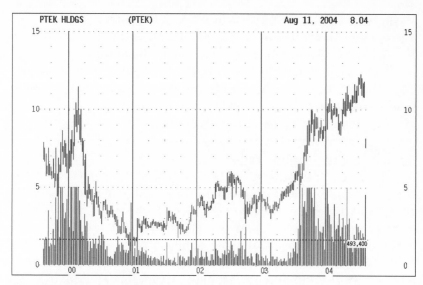

FIGURE 12.1 Ptek Holdings price chart.

and would ultimately show the ability to convert revenue to earnings and allow for expanding margins and growing profitability.

On August 7, 2003, Ptek Holdings announced the pricing of an offering of $75 million of 5 percent five-year convertible subordinated notes due in 2008. The press release stated that the notes were sold to qualified institutional buyers pursuant to Rule 144A under the Securities Act of 1933 as amended. In addition, certain persons in offshore transactions relying on Regulation S also purchased the offering. In essence, that press release announced to the world that the company had done a PIPE offering of convertible subordinated notes. The press release indicated that the notes were convertible under certain circumstances into the company's standard stock at a conversion rate of 149.4 shares per $1,000 of principal amount. That equaled a conversion price of approximately $6.69 per share. At the time, the common stock of the company was trading at about $5.50 a share, so the $6.69 conversion price represented a conversion premium of 18 percent. This indicated that institutional investors believed that the potential return on the common stock would be no less than 18 percent, based on the trading premium for which they negotiated upon the pricing of the securities. On August 21, the company filed a registration rights agreement between Ptek Holdings and CIBC World

Markets, an affiliate of UBS Securities, as the initial purchasers of the 5 percent convertible subordinated notes.

For purposes of micro cap analysis, UBS Securities would be considered a technical investor, and it's likely that these convertible subordinated notes went into one of its hedge fund vehicles. It would also be safe to assume that at the time, the time horizon on these notes, although having a useful life through August 2008, would for practical purposes be shorter than the five years indicated by the registration rights agreement.

In part, the company used the proceeds to fund several acquisitions of complementary business lines and fund several joint ventures with other service providers that would provide increased revenue for the company. The year 2003 was solidly profitable for the company, with the real profitability starting with the June 2003 quarter. However, sales began to increase with the September and December quarters, along with real net income, with the company showing $.42 of adjusted gap earnings for the year ended December 2003.

Since the August 2003 offering of convertible subordinated debentures, Ptek Holding stock has increased in value from approximately $5.50 per share to approximately $11.00 per share, showing about 100 percent appreciation over the time period.

On June 14, 2004, Ptek Holdings announced that all outstanding 5 percent convertible subordinated notes due in 2008 would be converted into approximately 12.7 million shares of common stock, all of which had been included in the company's diluted shares outstanding. As a condition of the conversion, Ptek would pay converting note holders accrued interest of approximately $1.4 million and also pay them a make-whole provision, essentially a prepayment penalty of approximately $16.3 million, which represents the net present value of future interest payments on the bonds.

During the first quarter of 2004, Ptek continued to perform strongly, with revenues increasing from $89 million in March 2003 to $105 million in March 2004. The company earned $.13 per common share on a fully diluted basis, an increase of 25 percent over the $.09 per share the company earned for the quarter ended March 2003. Since 2003, five well-known research organizations have elected to begin coverage on Ptek Holdings, including CIBC World Markets, which were the initial issuers of the convertible subordinated debt, and Morgan Keegan, a well-known regional brokerage firm. This is just a brief example of the private investment and public equities transactional activity that takes place in the capital markets. These types of transactions are worth scrutinizing in order to determine whether there is an opportunity available as a private micro cap investor. The addition of capital allows companies like Ptek Holdings to continue executing their business plans, along with increasing equity capitalization through ongoing conversion of convertible securities, all of which points to positive future valuation potential for the company.

CHAPTER 13

A Framework for Investor Action

This chapter will attempt to answer the following questions:

- How can you get started in micro cap investing?
- What should you consider when looking for micro cap opportunities?

There are two ways that investors can get started investing in micro caps. The simple and quickest way to get started is through a micro cap mutual fund or a money manager that specializes in micro cap portfolios. (More on this subject later.) The other way to get started is to analyze and select micro cap stocks for your own portfolio. For investors with the time and patience, this activity can be a rewarding contributor to the portfolio. Let's recap some important items to keep in mind when considering micro caps.

As Chapter 1 discussed, micro cap companies are publicly traded stocks with a market capitalization of $500 million or less. These companies have historically represented over 50 percent of all currently reporting publicly traded companies. There are at present more than 4,100 companies that meet this simple criterion. The opportunity lies in the fact that very few of these companies have any meaningful research coverage from Wall Street analysts or institutional investors. This allows you, as an individual investor, to research and analyze a large group of companies that are not closely monitored by large groups of investors. The opportunity is that a diligent analyst can discover and develop an information advantage over other investors. This can create the opportunity to invest in small public companies well ahead of the time when the information is widely recognized by other investors. These are the emerging companies that will be of great interest to a vast legion of professional small cap managers as they climb to market capitalizations that exceed $500 million. Companies such as Amazon.com started as micro cap opportunities.

The entire concept of an information advantage is discussed in Chapter 2. It revolves around the notion that markets are efficient. The chapter does not dispute the idea of the efficient market, which is well documented in academic literature. However, it does point to studies that suggest that in the short term, capital markets can be somewhat inefficient. And the smaller the capitalization of a company, the more likely it is that some level of market inefficiency exists. There is no unified theory to explain this phenomenon, but it can be partially explained by the principal agent problem that exists in private-venture capital transactions. This book concludes that micro cap stocks have some unique characteristics that are a result of their size. Like their larger capitalization publicly traded cousins, micro caps live within the boundaries of efficient market theory but behave slightly differently than their larger cousins. When compared to larger cap stocks, micro caps do not seem to reflect all available information as efficiently as larger cap public companies. This results in higher expected returns and higher volatility than large stocks. But the higher returns more than compensate for the added volatility. This leads us to the theory that there can be an information advantage available to diligent micro cap investors because the micro cap sector is less efficient in the speed at which it reflects information. If this were true, EMT would be called into question.

However, when comparing the micro cap investment sector to venture capital investing, the EMT inconsistencies within micro caps can be reconciled when considered in light of the principal agent venture capital model. This suggests that micro caps are a sector unto themselves. The sector has many of the elements of larger capitalization stocks as well as many characteristics of venture capital investments. In many ways, the micro cap sector is a bridge between the public equity markets and the private venture capital markets, and it displays the unified characteristics of both.

These unified characteristics are discussed in more detail in Chapter 3. There is no doubt that over time smaller stocks provide larger investment returns than bigger stocks. This is a function of the capital asset pricing model, which suggests that the more risk an investor undertakes, the more potential return is required. In the framework of the CAPM, investors are more than adequately rewarded for risks undertaken in micro cap stocks. This suggests that there is an opportunity to capture some excess return, or "alpha," in the micro cap asset class.

The data suggest that micro caps behave in part like venture capital investments, Chapter 4 examines how these investments might fit into the portfolio of the small investor as a substitute for the venture capital asset class due to their similar return profile. This chapter looks at the portfolio contribution and volatility of a theoretical investment portfolio as micro cap stocks are added and concludes that micro caps have a positive impact on the typical diversified portfolio, suggesting that an allocation of 5 percent to 20 percent in micro caps could be considered prudent over long-term time horizons.

As an individual investor making micro cap selections for an existing portfolio, an allocation of 5 percent is likely a good place to start. There should be a minimum target of 20 to 25 stocks within the portfolio, and they should be diversified across different industries to help spread the risk in the portfolio. As an individual investor, you don't need to make all the investments at once, but you could begin by selecting one or two new names each month until your portfolio is completely constructed. This strategy allows the investor to dollar-cost-average into the micro cap arena and further control the risk.

The next question is what to look for when selecting micro caps. If the principal agent relationship holds true, there are two groups of investors whose actions should be closely monitored when screening for micro cap opportunities. Company insiders who are the principals of the transaction are the first group to watch, and knowledgeable institutional investors who are the agents in venture capital theory are the other group to watch.

Observing the actions of these groups is relatively simple in the public capital markets because they are much more transparent, and therein exists the opportunity to gain an information advantage.

The buying and selling patterns of the key management team can be a stunning leading indicator of a company's future prospects. Who is in a better position to make a critical evaluation about the future business prospects of a company? The key management team will have firsthand knowledge of the day-to-day operations of the company and how it is progressing. In addition, the insiders have a keen awareness of the current valuation of the company. Who better to make an informed principal agent decision about the current value and future prospects of the company than the existing key management personnel? The pattern of their buying and selling can be a very powerful indicator of future stock performance. These material insiders are required to disclose their purchase and sale decisions to the public at large in a timely manner through filings with the SEC. The review of these filings can be a powerful tool for screening the micro cap universe for investment opportunities.

These insider trades can be monitored by reviewing the daily online filings made at the SEC through the agency's web site at edgar.gov, or an individual can subscribe to a service that compiles insider trading data such as insidertrader.com or the Thomson Financial Network at thomsoninvest.net. These are just two of the many sites that provide recent compilations of insider trading data.

A careful review of the company's recent public filings with the SEC will then help the investor to develop a theory on what catalyst has created buying interest on the part of management. Chapter 6 presents a suggested due diligence list of the data that an investor should review prior to making an investment. The top 10 items are:

1. Federal regulatory filings made by the company
2. Competitors of the company
3. Customers of the company
4. Suppliers to the company
5. Industry trade associations

6. Sell-side research analysts
7. Buy-side research analysts
8. Newspapers, magazines, and other publications
9. Internet searches
10. Briefs and related legal documents filed in public lawsuits

These easily available documents will help formulate a picture of the company, the industry, and the competitive landscape of the business.

After doing some homework, the list of potential companies should begin to take shape. Chapter 7 discusses how micro cap valuations differ from those of large capitalization stocks. The key thing to understand is that micro caps will normally look very cheap or very expensive when comparing them with the valuation of similar companies that are larger in market capitalization. This is driven primarily by the industry in which the micro cap exists and where the economy is within the economic cycle.

Academic research as well as studies done by Uniplan Consulting, LLC, our financial research affiliate, have indicated that some screening variables are generally more useful than others for the purposes of finding micro cap opportunities. There are three relevant financial analysis techniques that will help potential micro cap investors screen out potential investment candidates for consideration for their portfolios. As mentioned, the valuation criteria most suitable for a given micro cap company will depend largely on the type of business the company engages in and the value of the company relative to its industry peers. The three financial items to examine are:

1. Price to book value
2. Price to free cash flow
3. Price to earnings

We call them the "holy trinity" and use them as our basic screening tools to begin our searches. Again, this is not meant to be an exhaustive list of valuation methods, but rather some general screening criteria that can help narrow the universe of micro cap companies into smaller groups for more rigorous analysis.

Chapters 8 through 12 examine, through the use of case studies, how all these various factors can be reviewed in the context of real micro cap companies, including a discussion about the newly emerging strategy of private investments in public equities (PIPEs). These case studies often have all the aforementioned elements in various dimensions. They are useful in reviewing a methodology for approaching micro cap analysis; however, they are by no means definitive. Different investors will arrive at varying conclusions about the same company. The companies that you select for your portfolio might be entirely different from those that another investor using similar techniques might select. This, in many ways, is the most interesting and unique aspect of micro cap investing.

CHAPTER 14

Micro Cap Fund Investing

This chapter will attempt to answer the following questions:

- How can you use mutual funds to get micro cap exposure in your portfolio?
- What should you consider when selecting a micro cap fund?

Not everyone wants to select stocks for their portfolio. This is particularly true of micro caps, where there is a much higher level of primary research required to make investments. These investors should consider a micro cap mutual fund as an alternative for their micro cap investment allocation. There is a proliferation of fund information available on the Internet. The following is a simple summary of information that should be considered when investing in a micro cap mutual fund.

The first question most investors normally ask is: How is the performance? That is a good question but should not be the last question asked when reviewing micro cap funds. To really know how well a fund is doing, compare the fund's returns to appropriate benchmarks. In this case, the Wilshire Micro Cap Index would be the easiest and most useful benchmark. Then, compare the fund's performance to that of other funds that invest in the micro cap securities. Over longer periods of time, a fund should add performance over the benchmark. In this category, the time period considered should be no less than three years, and five years would be a better minimum because of the longer time horizon associated with micro cap investing. For a similar period, you should also consider how the fund's performance stacks up against that of other, similar funds. It is important to note that the funds should be similar because not all funds within a category are always comparable. A micro cap value style fund might look as though its performance is not good relative to a micro cap fund that invests in emerging technology stocks, but this should be considered when investing in a given fund. This goes to the issue of volatility—some funds are more volatile than others. As discussed earlier, the riskier the investment, the greater the expected return. In micro cap stocks, the risk is large, but the return expectations are large, too. But also remember that the greater the risk, the greater the potential for loss. Some micro cap managers have a penchant for more risk than others. Those who take on a lot of risk expect a greater return from their investments, but they don't always get it. Conversely, some managers are willing to give up the potential for large gains in return for a less bumpy ride. Consider a fund's volatility in light of the return it produces. Two funds with equal returns might not be equally attractive investments; one could be far more volatile than the other.

Nevertheless, it is important to be certain that no matter what a fund's return, the manager of the fund is the manager that produced the return. Keep in mind that funds are only as good as the people behind them. It is the fund managers who make the investments. Because the fund manager is the person responsible for a fund's performance, knowing who's calling the shots and how long he or she has been doing it is essential to selecting a micro cap fund. Make sure that the manager who built the majority of the fund's record is still the one in charge. Managers change with some frequency—particularly good managers—so it is important to do your homework on them.

As with researching a micro cap stock, there are some easily obtained documents you will need to research a fund. There are three valuable fund documents:

1. The prospectus
2. The statement of additional information (SAI)
3. The annual report

When you request an information kit from a mutual fund, you normally are sent a prospectus and the most recent shareholder report. These are also available online through the EDGAR site. Read them, because they are a wealth of information. Here's what you need from the prospectus and the statement of additional information.

The prospectus tells you how to open an account (including minimum-investment requirements), how to purchase or redeem shares, and how to contact shareholder services. There are six things you absolutely need to know about a fund before you decide to buy shares in the first place.

1. *Investment objective.* The investment objective is the mutual fund's investment mandate. Make sure it is a micro cap fund. Funds that can invest up to $1 billion in market capitalization often call themselves micro cap or mini cap funds. For our purposes, funds that focus on companies that are smaller than $500 million in market cap are preferred. Investment objectives can be notoriously vague, so a careful reading of the strategy section is important.

2. *Strategy.* The prospectus also describes the types of stocks and/or bonds and other securities in which the fund may invest, but it does *not* list the exact investments that the fund owns. The strategy section should spell out what kinds of companies the manager looks for, such as small, fast-growing firms or low P/E firms. If the fund can invest in foreign securities, the prospectus says so. Most restrictions on what the fund can invest in are also usually listed.

3. *Risks.* This section may be the most important one in the prospectus. Every investment has risks associated with it, and a prospectus must explain these risks. Because micro cap investing is of higher risk than most other investing, you can expect this section to be fairly long. It is important to not take any risks that may be associated with the manager's particular style. For example, some managers invest in very illiquid stocks that may not trade every day. This is a form of liquidity risk that could have an impact on the fund's daily price or net asset value (NAV).

4. *Expenses.* Everyone needs to get paid, and it costs money to invest in a mutual fund. Different funds have different fees.

There is a table at the front of every prospectus that makes it easy to compare the cost of one fund with that of another. You'll find the sales commission the fund charges, if any, for buying or selling shares. The prospectus also tells you, in percentage terms, the amount deducted from the fund's return each year to pay for management fees and operational costs. Micro cap investing is relatively labor intensive, so the expense ratio of micro cap funds tends to be higher than that of other types of stock funds. Keep this in mind, because micro cap fund expenses can often exceed 2 percent per year.

5. *Past performance.* As the saying goes, past performance is not indicative of future results. It can, however, give you an idea of how consistent a fund's returns have been. A chart headed "Financial Highlights" or "Per Share Data Table" provides the fund's total return for each of the past 10 years, along with other useful information about fund performance. It also breaks out the fund's income distributions and provides the year-end NAV. Some prospectuses include additional return information in the form of a bar chart that illustrates the fund's calendar returns for the past 10 years. This chart is a good way to get a handle on the magnitude of a fund's ups and downs over time. The prospectus may also use a growth of $10,000 mountain graph, a table comparing the fund's performance to indexes, or other benchmarks to present return information.

6. *Management.* The management section explains the people who will be investing the money in the fund. The fund should tell you the name and experience of the fund manager or managers. However, some funds simply list "management team" or some other less-than-helpful description. If that's the case, consult the fund's statement of additional information or the annual report to see if more specific information is given there. It is also possible to call the fund itself or check out the fund family's web site. If this still does not yield the names and tenure of the team, then it is a likely bet that you should avoid the fund. If the prospectus does name names, check how long the current manager has been running the fund to be sure that the fund's past record was not achieved under someone else. Also, it is worthwhile to find out whether the

manager has run other funds or is currently running other funds. A look at those funds could give you some clues about the manager's investment style and past success.

There are three ways in which funds can be managed:

1. *The single-manager approach.* With this model, there is one person who takes primary responsibility for making the fund's investment decisions. The manager normally does not do all the research, trading, and decision making without help from others. So it is important to remember that the single manager may be the sole decision maker but is not likely the sole idea generator.

2. *The management team.* This concept was popularized by families like American Century, Scudder, and Putnam. With this model, two or more people work together to choose investments. The level of one team member's involvement or responsibilities can be difficult to gauge. Sometimes there's a lead manager who is the final investment arbiter, while other times it is more of a democracy with regard to portfolio selections.

3. *The multiple-manager system.* The fund's assets are divided among a number of managers who work independently of each other. This model is not seen very often in the micro cap arena. American Funds is one of the biggest fund families using this approach, but they do not have a micro cap product. Multiple managers are more common with subadvised funds, such as Forward Funds, the CDC Nvest funds, and the American Advantage Group, in which the fund company hires managers from other companies to run the fund.

Funds run by teams are often less affected by manager changes than funds run by only one person. But that's true only if the fund really was run in a team fashion, whereby decisions are truly democratic. Conversely, then, manager changes can be a problem for

- Single-manager funds
- Funds run by very active managers who've proved to be adept stock pickers or traders

- Good funds from families that aren't strong overall, or from fund families that lack other strong funds with a similar investment style
- Funds in categories such as micro caps where the range of possible returns is very wide

This is why it is important to know managers and manager tenures in the instances of micro cap funds.

Although the prospectus is packed with great information, it shouldn't be your sole source of data on a fund. A fund's statement of additional information contains very detailed information about the fund's inner workings. Be sure to ask for this document specifically—funds routinely send out prospectuses and annual reports, but SAIs are often not distributed unless specifically asked for. The SAI often provides far more detail than the prospectus about what the fund can and cannot invest in. The SAI also is usually the place where you can find out who represents your interests on the fund's board of directors and how much they are paid. Finally, you can find more details about your fund's expenses here, including brokerage fees paid by the fund and a breakdown of where 12b-1 fees go, if the fund charges them.

Once you invest in a micro cap fund, it is important to monitor the fund. Mutual funds can also lose their edge. A good fund may not always be a good fund. Funds do change. Sometimes their performance slips or their managers leave or their strategies evolve away from their mission. That is why funds need to be monitored. Here are some of the red flags to watch out for as you monitor your fund. These items may signal that a change is on the way.

As funds attract new investors and grow larger, their returns often become sluggish, weighed down by too many assets. They lose their potency and their returns revert to the average for their group. This is particularly the case in the micro cap sector. Good performance attracts money that makes it harder for the fund to maintain performance—an ugly paradox. The best funds will stop accepting money from new investors when their assets grow too large, but greed overcomes most funds and they don't stop. That explains why so many once-hot funds become mediocre.

The mutual fund industry is littered with the bodies of small-growth funds or funds whose strategies involved a lot of trading that put up terrific numbers by buying fast-growing small-company stocks and quickly selling them when their growth stalled. The performance of these funds drew lots of attention from investors, and their asset base swelled. Returns slowed because the managers just couldn't execute their fast-trading, supergrowth strategy with so many assets under management.

The second side effect of asset growth is that fund managers often alter their strategies to accommodate asset growth. Some simply buy more stocks, buy larger companies, or trade less. No matter what they do, though, they make some kind of change. And as a shareholder, you need to be aware of the change and consider whether this alteration impacts the fund's ability to truly be a micro cap fund.

Finally you should be sure to rebalance your portfolio. Say you originally constructed a portfolio of 50 percent stocks, 40 percent bonds, and 10 percent micro caps. If left alone over a 10-year period, that portfolio could easily grow into a blend of 64 percent stocks, 14 percent bonds, and 22 percent micro caps. Presumably, you set up your original allocation to match your needs and risk tolerance. If neither has changed, your allocation shouldn't, either. For example, if stocks take over your portfolio, as they do in the example, your returns may rise but so will your risk. The best way to return the portfolio to the original risk level is by buying and selling funds until you reach your original allocation. That's what rebalancing is all about. It forces you to take profits when certain assets are outperforming and to reinvest in those same assets when they are underperforming. Here are some simple guidelines for rebalancing.

- *Don't rebalance too often.* You needn't worry about rebalancing every quarter, or even every year. Studies have found that investors who rebalanced their investments at 18-month intervals reaped many of the same benefits as those who rebalanced more often. Investors who rebalance less frequently save themselves unnecessary labor and, in the case of taxable investments, there can be some tax savings, too. As mentioned, rebalancing requires reducing the winners, which means realizing capital gains and, for the taxable investor, paying taxes. Although you should monitor your mutual fund portfolio on a monthly basis at a minimum, resist the urge to rebalance too often unless one of your funds has significantly changed its strategy.

- *When you rebalance pay attention to the stock/bond split.* Your bond investments are vital to keeping your portfolio's risk in line. Because bonds don't generally move in sync with your stock investments, a simple strategy of restoring your bond fund allocation to its original weightings every 18 months will help to lower your portfolio's overall risk.

- *Rebalance micro cap and other focused styles by the numbers, not the calendar.* Like any good concept, rebalancing can be taken to extremes. Some investors follow very detailed asset allocations that involve very specific targets, such as a 20 percent micro cap target. They then rebalance when the style-specific allocations get out of whack, as well as when their overall stock/bond split goes awry. When it comes to subasset classes or investment styles, studies by Morningstar Mutual Fund Advisory have found that a policy of readjusting whenever one style takes up one-fourth more or one-fourth less than its original portfolio position is most effective. For example, you'd want to rebalance when the micro cap fund to which you devoted 20 percent of your portfolio rises to 25 percent or sinks to 15 percent. This allows for the longer time horizon required by some asset classes to be realized.

- *Use new money to rebalance.* A longtime strategy of financial advisors is to counsel taxable investors that when adding fresh dollars to their portfolios, they should add to their laggards to avoid the tax consequences of selling their winners. Absent new money to put to work, consider having your funds' income and capital gains distributions paid into a money market account and using that cash for rebalancing.

Whether you invest in micro cap mutual funds, in separately managed micro cap accounts, or directly in micro cap stocks, the strategies in this book should help the micro cap investor manage the risks and derive the benefits of making big returns by investing in small companies.

Index